Economic Club

Family Budgets

Being the Income and Expenses of twenty-eight British Households.

1891-1894

Economic Club

Family Budgets
Being the Income and Expenses of twenty-eight British Households. 1891-1894

ISBN/EAN: 9783337151393

Printed in Europe, USA, Canada, Australia, Japan

Cover: Foto ©ninafisch / pixelio.de

More available books at **www.hansebooks.com**

FAMILY BUDGETS: BEING THE INCOME AND EXPENSES OF TWENTY-EIGHT BRITISH HOUSEHOLDS. 1891-1894.

COMPILED FOR THE ECONOMIC CLUB, WITH AN INTRODUCTION.

LONDON:
P. S. KING & SON,
12 & 14, KING STREET,
WESTMINSTER, S.W.
1896.

CONTENTS.

INTRODUCTION.

THIS little book is the result of an effort to study family life in Great Britain through details of family expenditure, and from this it takes its title ."Family Budgets." It follows humbly, and at some distance, in the footsteps of Le Play. Being the work of several hands it lacks uniformity of treatment. In exchange it gains, perhaps, something in vividness and variety.

It sets forth its wares to meet the taste of two different classes of readers, or at least appeals to very different sides of any reader's mind. As the outcome of an " Economic Club " it puts in the forefront tables which bring together and lay open for comparison the numerical, economic facts, and from these it leaves the reader or student to draw his own conclusions on the special points that may interest him. Many more than twenty-eight Budgets would be requisite to justify complete, self-sustained, unquestionable conclusions ; more questions are suggested than answered ; but the material, so far as it goes, is good.

Beyond this strictly statistical interest the short stories which precede the tables, and to which the tables serve as an index, give us a warm human interest in the lives described. The Budgets are not confined to one locality or to one class. They extend from Sussex to Scotland—from London to St. Ives. Town and country conditions are represented as well as many varieties of circumstances, from the middle class comfort to the pinch of great poverty.

It may be well to give a short history of the steps by which this collection has been brought together.

In 1891, at a meeting of the Economic Club, the subject of Workmen's Budgets was introduced ; and a proposal that the members should, under the general auspices of the Club, collect such Budgets was favourably received and referred to the Executive, by which a Special Sub-Committee was subsequently appointed.

A few weeks later a specimen Budget (now No. 1a in the series printed), was prepared and circulated among the members. In July, 1892, a circular letter was addressed to them, accompanied by a schedule of questions and instructions. Both were distributed in the first place among the members, but also through them amongst a certain number of friends likely to co-operate. In the letter the importance of choosing families that were as typical as possible and whose accuracy might be counted upon, both in filling up the schedule and in keeping the accounts, was emphasized. It was also urged that the accounts should be kept day by day, and item by item, for as long a period as possible, and in no case for less than a month. In the schedule twenty-seven questions were enumerated and a specimen of the method of keeping the accounts was added.

In all, about thirty-eight Budgets have been sent in to the Committee, about half the number being accompanied by a descriptive monograph. As was to be expected, the material was found to possess very different degrees of value, and a few sets of accounts were rejected as being useless for the purpose of the Club. Eventually it was decided to print tabular results of twenty-eight Budgets, in the majority of cases with brief notes on the families, and in seven cases with the monographs in full, these last being selected from those that had most intrinsic value and were most representative in character. In some cases, it is to be noted that only cursory schedule notes on the figures and the family to which they refer were sent in, and these had to be thrown into connected form. The whole of this work of amplification as well as that of abstracting the longer monographs, which it was decided not to print in full, and the still more laborious task of summarising the accounts, as shown in the tables, was undertaken by Miss Edith Collet and Miss Robertson, to whom the Club is greatly indebted for the time and trouble they have given to the work.

The Budgets that have been printed, including eight from the Metropolitan area, nine from Provincial towns, and eleven from the rural districts, have been sent in by ten members and three non-members of the Club.

Although the method of account-keeping in the various families has varied somewhat, it has been found possible, with rare exceptions, to tabulate the accounts in accordance with a uniform plan. Most of the figures in the raw material reached the Committee in the small account books in which the items had been originally entered by a member of the family.

The monographs, however, show a much greater variety of form than the accounts, and vary from the brief notes appended to the schedules, which, indeed, hardly deserve the name of monographs, to a full description of the family. A well-defined class of monographs will be observed by all readers in the three cases (Nos. 4, 5 and 15) in which the text has been written, not by the observer or compiler, but by the head of the family himself.

The general plan of the tables will explain itself on examnination. The first (A) is a general summary of the composition, income and expenditure of the family, with particulars concerning the period covered by the accounts; the second (B) is an analysis showing the weekly average expenditure on food and drink; the third (C) gives a corresponding analysis of the weekly average expenditure for all articles other than food and drink, including such headings as rent, boots, recreation, etc., and the fourth (D) shows the percentage of certain selected and significant items: (*a*) to the total weekly expenditure, and (*b*) to the total weekly expenditure on food and drink.

The Budgets, in spite of their imperfections, will be found very fruitful and suggestive. Sometimes they will be found so from the light which they throw upon some economic point, the importance of which is already well known; sometimes, however, they direct attention to the very existence of some question which is not likely to have been previously under our notice, and which will be recognised, perhaps for the first time, as deserving further attention. It is often as useful to have an important economic point suggested to us for further consideration, as it is to secure a general answer to a problem already formulated, the existence and importance of which is present to the mind.

Some of the points, framed as questions, to which the Budgets direct attention, and to which some of them give partial answers, are the following :—

 1. To what extent is the elimination of the small general shop in process? What method of distribution is taking its

place ? Is it, in the country, the co-operative store or the
larger firm of the neighbouring town that reaches its customers
by the van or the Parcels Post; or, in the city, the larger
and more attractive establishment of the neighbouring main
street ? To what extent is this normal effect of competition,
to " eliminate the unnecessary middleman," hindered by
(*a*) convenience; and (*b*) the prevailing system of credit ?
(*cf.* Budgets Nos. 7 and 27).

2. To what extent is loss to the small consumer*caused
by the necessity of purchasing in small quantities? The
widespread and well-founded notion is, that the loss is considerable and inevitable, but such a passage as the following
reminds us that there is another side to the question: in
monograph No. 1, for instance, the compiler, who states elsewhere that the only commodity in which the wife thinks much
loss is incurred through her small purchases is coal, writes as
follows :—

> The children are not old enough to earn money. The boy of eight is,
> however, sent to do small errands. He is found to receive sympathetic
> attention when he has a farthing or half-penny to lay out; while his
> father and mother would often be told that orders of such small value
> cannot be executed. When there is no definite measure for a " ha'porth "
> his parents think he " gets the benefit of the doubt."

There is also a widespread opinion among housewives
that the danger of greater consumption arising from the
possession in the house of large quantities is almost certain
to follow. This is most likely to happen in the case of
attractive articles of food unless the wife is careful in
management. One case, *e.g.*, has come before the notice of
the Committee in which the wife intentionally bought very
small quantities of jam because of the rapidity with which her
husband made it disappear if a larger quantity were put upon
the table.

3. To what extent does the want of comfort in lodgings
lead to hasty or early marriages ? In two cases at least
(Nos. 1 and 4) the heads of the families were hurried into
marriage by the discomfort of living in lodgings, and the
compiler of No. 1 in a note (page 22) states that London
workmen, when spoken to on the unwisdom of marrying
before due provision has been made to avoid distress, not
infrequently say that they are led into precipitate marriage

owing to the discomfort and swindling to which they are subjected in their lodgings.

4. To what extent is the marked absence of supplementary earnings* in comparison with the extent with which they figure in the Budgets of continental families, due to the absence of the habit and custom among our own people of seeking for such resources; and how far, when land is necessary in order to secure them, is their absence due to the special difficulty of securing it in this country?

5. On the habits of thrift, on the extent to which, and the forms in which, the Friendly Society System operates throughout the country, a considerable amount of interesting fact may be collected from the Budgets. But most significant in this connection is perhaps the light they throw upon the attitude of humble families towards the Poor Law, and the widespread prevalence they illustrate of the habits of sturdy self-dependence.

6. On the more general question of the composition of working-class dietaries but little further light is thrown. The detailed accounts suggest a much greater variety than do the summaries given in the printed tables, and this becomes still more apparent when the details and the number of articles consumed are compared with, let us say, any corresponding Budget of the last century. Important questions are suggested as to the extent to which the expenditure is intelligent, and as to how far the elementary principles of domestic economy are understood by the wives of wage-earners. But generalizations on the character of their expenditure and still less on the prevailing Standard of Comfort cannot be hazarded upon the insufficient data that we possess.

In the same way very little fresh light is thrown upon the question of the *real value* of earnings. One important poin however in this connection is abundantly emphasized, viz that the real value to the individual family will by no means be altogether determined by any ruling range of prices, but also to a very great extent by the habits and capacities of the wife.

---

* It may be noted that, while particulars of income are always difficult to secure, this item of supplementary earnings is one that is especially likely to be omitted.

7. On the question as to where economies are most likely to be practised when means are more than usually straitened, a careful examination of Budgets Nos. 1 and 26 will throw some light, and a useful comparison on this point might be made between the Budgets of some of the more well-to-do families and those of the more indigent.

8. Concrete instances are constantly brought to our notice in the following pages of the importance of mobility as a means of securing industrial experience; and also of the importance of distinguishing between that form of mobility that indicates enterprise and increased economic efficiency and that which indicates shiftlessness—the absence of the power of persistent application, and which leads to economic waste. The first of these points has far-reaching importance and has much more than an ethical significance. In one aspect, for instance, it touches the whole question of apprenticeship and training, and the widespread opinion in many branches of the Building Trades in London in favour of " picking up " a knowledge of a trade—of going first as a boy and then as an improver, and of moving from shop to shop in order to secure the advantages of various experiences, forms one, but of course only one, of the obstacles to the extension of systematic training among the younger workers in this group of trades.

9. As regards the incidence of indirect taxation, very little information can be obtained from the Budgets, and a calculation of the amount paid by the various heads of the families, if based upon the figures of the Budgets, would, doubtless, to some considerable extent, be misleading.*

10. The table of percentages (D) shows interesting and suggestive differences in the ratio of certain items to the total expenditure, but little further light is thrown upon the question as to the extent to which the varying ratio, as, for instance, of rent or food, to total expenditure can be reduced to any general law.

In several of the preceding paragraphs it has been admitted that as regards many special points, the statistics and the descriptive

---

* In some cases when particulars of earnings were not forthcoming, the independent expenditure of the husband is not stated, and in other cases his private disbursements in tobacco, beer and spirits are probably omitted, being included, perhaps, under the head of " pocket money " and " other expenses."

material of the Budgets are of secondary importance. On the real meaning of the family, however; on the importance of the family life and the strength of the family tie; and on the strong instincts that make the family still the fundamental social fact and the true economic unit, the value of the Budgets seems to us to be of quite another order. Almost every detail given may be said to help in increasing this value. Our material has been collected, it is true, in a somewhat unsystematic way, but, on these general questions, it is none the less scientific and light-giving.

It may be said, indeed, that while similarity in the method of presenting the accounts is an essential, variety in description is at least a desideratum. The vitality of the collection of Budgets is secured by this variety. By its help we are enabled in some degree to measure the influences at work in the individual family; to detect its idiosyncrasies; to judge whether the dominant forces within it make for continuous life or for disintegration—for economic strength or for weakness and waste. A small collection of pictures giving us such insight has been secured, in some respects, in a very admirable form. Our records, it is true, do not cover a sufficiently long period of time to make us feel that we have much more than an instantaneous picture of any individual family. The material affords a basis, however, upon which, if time and patience were given to it, a collection might be formed that would have, not more human interest than ours, but considerably greater scientific value.

In forming such a collection it is probable that the method of enquiry here adopted must, on the whole, be followed, *i.e.*, that it must be *intensive* in form, the investigators contenting themselves with a comparatively small number of families, and not endeavouring to cover the greater number that could, it is true, be secured by the adoption of the *extensive* method. On the latter plan, while a larger number of particulars might be obtained, the more imposing statistical array would be comparatively barren of teaching, because lacking the material needed to place the unit of the household in the framing of home, of training, of industrial environment, of habit, of influence and of character that its proper comprehension would demand. We have secured a series of pictures framed in a way that gives us at least some insight into actuality, and it is in this fact, it seems, that the chief value of the Budgets is to be found.

In conclusion we would refer to certain general lines of criticism to which the Budgets will certainly be subjected. Some are obvious. For instance :—

  1. The absence of any Budget of many important repre-sentative classes of the community ;

  2. In many cases the incompleteness of the analysis and enumeration (*e.g.*, we have frequently no account of incomings, and in only one case is a detailed record given of the furni-ture—that important gauge of the persistent well-being of the family).

  3. The small number of Budgets given.

The recognition of the validity of such lines of criticism will guard us against any attempt to draw wide generalisations from the small array of facts and figures that we possess.

One objection that is often advanced against Budgets is sure to be raised against the collection of the Club, viz., that as soon as accounts are kept at the request of another person, no matter how trusted the person may be, they are sure to be affected by the knowledge that they will be seen by other people ; that little luxuries will be omitted, or will perhaps appear under the head of some necessary : boots, for instance, may figure for even more than their normally large proportion as an item of expenditure ; and we may perhaps look in vain for the cost of personal indulgences, and still more in vain for that of graver extravagancies.*

Doubtless there are a certain number of omissions of this kind ; and in looking down such columns as " Alcoholic Drinks " and " Tobacco " one is certainly struck by the abstemiousness and even the self-denying lives that most of the adult males, whose expendi-ture is in most cases supposed to have been given in full, must have led. But two points are pertinent and weaken the importance of the criticism.

  1. The accounts are probably in all cases those of respect-able folk ; the Budgets of the ne'er-do-weels, be they rich or

---

* Sometimes the risk of omissions and concealment may be increased by the very intimacy of the person for whom the accounts are kept. In certain cases it might be worth considering whether the accounts might not be passed on unread by, let us say, the friend who has collected them to the unknown member of some economic club.

poor, will always be difficult to secure. From the general character of the families, therefore, the margin of expense for which there will be motive for concealment will, by hypothesis, be small.

2. The accounts of the respectable family are most useful and most representative. The consciously wasteful and extravagant expenditure of the rank and file of the wage-earning classes may be safely said to represent, not indeed a negligible quantity, but certainly a small proportion of their total annual outgoings.

This opinion is corroborated by a volume of accounts in the possession of a member of the club. The period covered by them exceeds ten years, and the record was kept entirely for private reasons without any idea of their being used for any scientific purpose. There is abundant internal evidence that any omissions are due to carelessness, and not to any motive of concealment.

The accounts are interspersed with occasional diary notes, and many of the pages throw a somewhat lurid light on the experiences of the young artizan who kept them, especially in the years immediately preceding his marriage. Expenses for cigars, visits to music halls, "sprees," presents to his lady-friends, "rows," and notes of the occasions (sometimes with and sometimes without a statement of their money cost), when he got "tight," are all recorded, and the whole statement is one of extraordinary frankness and freedom.

But even these accounts in the years of his greatest extravagance show a large balance on the side of what may be called reasonable expenditure. There are, indeed, some weeks when his "sprees" were very costly; and when wasteful expenditure exceeded that of every other kind. But these are quite the exception. Examination shows that he may fairly be said to have "thrown away" about 15 per cent. of his earnings during these early years of his working life. He was earning about 36/- per week.

In making all reasonable allowance, therefore, for intentional omissions (and the Cambridge Budgets, it may be mentioned, were not kept for the Club, but quite independently for their own practical use in house-keeping) we may fairly say that the strong impression left behind, after a perusal of these Budgets, that the pictures they present are *true* ones, is well-founded ; and it may well be urged that, even if there be some defects, a modicum of truth has still its own independent value. We cannot, in enquiries of this kind, expect to be able to give " the truth, the whole truth, and nothing but the truth." All we can hope to arrive at is the truth, nearly all the truth, and very little but the truth, and this has been secured.

CHARLES BOOTH,
ERNEST AVES,   *Committee.*
HENRY HIGGS,

MONOGRAPHS.

NOTES ON THE FAMILIES:

MONOGRAPHS AND ABSTRACTS.

1.*

[LONDON.]   1891.

[BY THE COMPILER.]

Jobbing Plumber, age 30.   *Children :* Boys, ages 8 and 5.
Wife   age 29.   *Girl,* age 3.

I.

THE HISTORY OF THE FAMILY.

History of the Family.—The man's parents were Londoners, but his father's mother was born in France. His home was unhappy, owing to the drinking habits of his father, and, as the eldest child, he was kept much at home to help his mother and look after the children, with the result that his education was much neglected. Nominally at school for four or five years, he was absent more than half the time. At the age of twelve he was glad to leave school, and start work as an errand boy. In this capacity he served 2 months with a greengrocer, 8 months with a linendraper, and 12 months at a china shop, returning next to the greengrocer. His mother now died, and he went to live with an aunt, and engaged himself at a low wage to a plumber. Having a natural liking for this work, and thinking his want of education would not seriously impede him in it, he deliberately chose it as his trade, soon picked it up, was entrusted with skilled work, and stayed with the same employer nearly 7 years. At this time his aunt died. Though he paid her for his lodging, he was " not too comfortable " with her ; but, when he removed to other lodgings, he found them much more uncomfortable.† He was now thrown out of work, through a quarrel with his foreman, and could get nothing to do for a fortnight. Having, however, saved £10 or £11, he married during this fortnight within a few weeks of his aunt's death.

The wife was born in London. She lost her father (a cabman) when she was very young, and went to the King Edward's Schools for destitute children at Southwark, a charitable institution, whence she was drafted at the age of 15 into domestic service as a general servant. This situation was so uncomfortable, that she left it at once for another. In all, she tried five places, remaining 3 years as nursemaid in one of them, and marrying from the last.

---

* The numbers correspond with those in Tables A, B, C, D.
† See Note (a), page 22.

Since his marriage, the man's employment has been marked by extreme irregularity and uncertainty.   When her first-born was 6 months old, the wife fell ill of bronchitis and required more nourishing food.   To obtain this, her husband, who had no work at the time, allowed the rent to fall in arrear 11s., when their home (worth about £5 to them) was distrained upon, and broken up. Since then, they have not been able to get on their legs again. On one occasion, when he lay ill for a month in St. Thomas's Hospital, his wife was forced to apply for out-door relief, having absolutely no resources.   The necessary steps of appearing before the Guardians, receiving the Overseer's visit, &c., were not surmounted for nearly a fortnight, when they were "almost starving."   They were allowed 2s. 6d. a week, and received this for two weeks.   Directly the husband came home convalescent, the relief stopped.   It has not been applied for except this once. The misfortune of the time, the tardiness of the relief, and the surliness of the Overseer, are looked back upon with some bitterness of recollection by the man, who is devoted to his wife and children.   Some months ago their fourth child, a boy of two months, died of inflammation of the lungs, on a cold day, when the last penny had run out, and there was no fire in the room. The loss of the child is keenly felt : they repine too, that the funeral was necessarily of the cheapest (30s.) and plainest.   As the man puts it ; " We could not have the little fall-things, wot shows respect."*   Neither trials in the past nor fears for the future have, however, broken down their honesty, cheerfulness, or self-respect.   The wife extorts the maximum of utility from their slender resources.   Her husband has no further aspiration than the hope of permanent and regular employment.   A good week, when it comes, clears off the debts and shadows of the bad, and provides for the time some satisfaction of the more urgent needs of clothing or substantial food which have been forced into abeyance.   Comfort arising from neatness of home and person is relatively high ; but the standard of this precarious living is so low, that it is difficult to conceive of a lower, apart from actual starvation.

Moral circumstances.—On Sunday afternoons the children are sent to a Wesleyan Sunday School.   In the evening they are put to bed early, and their parents go to the Wesleyan Chapel "to pass away an hour."   They incur no expenses in these respects.   The man does not smoke; neither he nor his wife drinks.   The family is orderly, truthful and honest ; but offers no soil for the cultivation of foresight in the direction of saving. Earnings are spent within the week.   The eldest boy is sent to the Board School at a cost of 3d. per week levied for each week during which he is at least once present.   Last winter he was ill for 11 weeks and rarely attended ; the fees were then remitted after his mother had been before the Local Managers.†

Hygiene.—The man is of strong constitution.   His only illness since marriage arose from lead poisoning, due to the inhalation of ingredients of colour on a day when he resumed

---

work with an empty stomach after two weeks enforced idleness.
This was the occasion of his transfer to the hospital. The demand
for beds led, as he asserts, to his premature discharge. Having
no money to pay his fare, he walked home (3 miles), and the
same night had two fits—his first and last attacks—attributed to
weakness and fatigue.

The wife was strong until after the birth of her first child, when,
endeavouring too soon to get about her work in the house, she
caught cold, which brought on a lung trouble, never since got rid
of. Her mother came to nurse her ; but the eviction of the family
(*see p.* 18) happening at the time, she was, through the kind offices
of her doctor's sister, sent the same day to a convalescent home at
Kilburn, and there kept for four weeks at 8/6 a week, her husband
ultimately bearing half the expense. The oldest boy is consumptive.
The family often lacks the warmth and nutrition necessary for the
preservation of health. In case of illness application is made to a
charitable dispensary which provides medical advice, medicine,
bandages, &c., to accepted patients, who must pay 1d. on each visit
on application, and find their own bottles. The doctor now attend-
ing the wife, spoke to a charitable lady of her want of coal during a
severe illness, and the want was supplied. A previous (charitable)
doctor, as already stated, interested his sister in this poor patient.

The children play in their school-yard, and sometimes in a
neighbouring park, but this is restricted by the fear of their parents
that they might get into bad company.

II.

ITS MEANS OF EXISTENCE.

Sources of Income.—The man describes himself as a three-
branch man. His main business is that of a jobbing plumber.
The usual wages of a London plumber are said to be 9d. an
hour, and the weekly hours of labour 56½ generally, in the suburbs,
53 in the " City," and large suburban firms. This plumber trusts
to his local connexion, and the information supplied by comrades,
for his jobs. When out of work he applies to firms, and sometimes
to likely householders. Other resources failing he tries to earn
a trifle as a porter at auction rooms, or wherever he can get
a job for the time. He is not deft at paper-hanging, and it took
him 14 hours to hang 9 pieces at 6d. a piece, with his own paste
(costing 2¾d.) His tools, worth about 5s., would cost 30s. to replace.
He is often unable to do a job because his tools have been pawned.
There is nothing else upon which he can raise a loan. The
interest charged is ¼d. in the 1s. for each month, and ½d. for the
pawn-ticket.

The wife is too delicate to do charing, or take in work. To
oblige an unmarried brother " who is rather particular," she
washes and mends his linen, but the 6d. a week which he sends in
payment does not cover the expense of mangling and washing
materials. She would like, she says, to do the work for nothing.
She makes the children's stockings and all their garments, except
the girl's dresses. She has a small sewing machine. But her main

contribution to the economy of the family is her very skilful house-keeping, which circumvents poverty by the most ingenious expedients.

The children are not old enough to earn money. The boy of eight is, however, sent to do the small errands. He is found to receive sympathetic attention when he has a farthing, or half-penny to lay out; while his father or mother would often be told that orders of such small value could not be executed. When there is no definite measure for a " ha'porth " his parents think he " gets the benefit of the doubt." He is also useful about the house, and, for his mother's health, lights the fire before she gets up; but complaint is made that he burns more wood in the process than a grown person would do.

The family has no credit, nor can it count upon the aid of relatives, except that at rare intervals it gets a cast garment, which the wife makes up. When they lost their baby, the man's brother, though actually out of work, " made " 30s. (*i.e.*, by pledging) and lent it to them to pay the funeral expenses. And the wife's mother, now dead, took in the man and his children when they were homeless. Last Christmas they received a 4-lb. joint of beef and ¼-lb. of tea from a lady at the chapel, who observed that they " used the place regular." The pleasures of memory as to this feast are still very vivid. The wife was recently discovered by an old fellow-servant, whose mistress now gives the man an occasional job, and his wife a few odd things, surplus food, a remnant of linen and the like. But the family receives no visits and conceals its privations; so that this spasmodic help does not always come at the best time.

Their last lines of defence are (i.) to fall back upon cheaper and scantier food; (ii.) to pawn. Neither resource will bear much strain.

III.

ITS MODE OF EXISTENCE.

Meals.—Breakfast 8.0 a.m.   Tea, bread and margarine or fat bacon.

Dinner 12.45.   Bread and margarine.   Two or three days a week, meat and vegetables, or fish.   On Sunday, when possible, suet pudding is added.

Tea 5 p.m.   Tea, bread and margarine.

There is never supper. The man takes a tin flask of tea with him in the morning, and warms it where he is working; he carries his bread and butter. His dinner, bread and cheese, or bread and a rasher of bacon, at an eating house costs 2d. or 4d. When he is working within easy distance he comes home to dinner. He complains that the children are given food between meals when they sometimes cry for it out of mere whim, though at other times they suffer real hunger.

The fat bacon, used instead of " butter," is melted in a frying-pan, and a slice of bread put into the pan to absorb the fat. The children are fond of this economic dish, which is nutritive and a change from " butter."

The eldest boy is sent before 7 a.m. to a neighbouring baker's, to buy bread baked two days earlier, and sold at a very low price, five twopenny loaves for 3d.* The baker's supply is, however, too small to be counted upon daily. Syrup is found to be cheaper than treacle because it is thinner and spreads further.

The only commodity in which the wife thinks much loss is incurred through her want of means is coal. This is bought at 14-lb. for 2d, though the price per ton is 19s., and per cwt. 1s. 2d. Block fuel is bought in emergencies, but it provokes her cough and is no saving. Asked whether Indian tea at 1s. 10d. would not yield more cups than dust at 1s. 2d., she replies that she is fanciful about her cup of tea, and finds the Indian tea too rough. When times are good a tin of Swiss milk is bought (3½d.) This is ample for a whole week; and on Sunday the children have suet pudding with Swiss milk spread upon it. Loaf sugar is never bought, the children would want pieces to eat.

Dwelling, Furniture, and Clothing. — The house is situated near Loughboro' Junction in the S.E. of London, in a neighbourhood thickly peopled by the lower middle class, by artisans of small regular earnings, railway servants, etc. This family occupies the top or second floor. Its two rooms are well-lighted and ventilated. The front room, looking upon a street of considerable width, is the living room of the family and the bedroom of the parents. The boys sleep in the back room, the girl on a bed-chair in the large room. There is no attachment to a particular dwelling. They have removed seven times in all. Their furniture is too trifling to make this process expensive or dangerous. They are anxious to remain here because the rent 4s. a week, is 6d. lower than their last lodging, and they could not expect to find equally good rooms elsewhere at the same rent. They find that householders object to poor families with young children as tenants. Their last residence was an undertenancy of a workman, who, himself, got into arrears and was evicted. They were obliged by the superior landlord to leave at the same time. They have a good water supply and sanitary accommodation. Trains run very near the top of the house. The immediate vicinity is cheerless and depressing.

The furniture and clothing are very scanty, but kept fairly (not perfectly) clean. The best room has a rough carpet, a few cheap prints, a chest of drawers, and a little American clock, which they have owned (if not possessed) ever since their marriage. Out of doors the man wears an overcoat, which is warm and conceals deficiency of other clothing. Indoors, or at work, the overcoat is removed, and reveals him in shirt sleeves. The bed-clothes, in like manner, are a thin counterpane, and little more.

Recreation.—The man plays a little upon the flute, mainly to amuse the children, in whom he finds his chief pleasure. Sitting, coatless, before the fire of an evening a boy on one knee and a girl on the other, he sings or whistles, and, as he says, "'as a game with 'em in my way." At 7.30 p.m. (having arisen at 7 a.m.) the children go to bed; and the man goes to his brother's to have a game of dominoes. These visits are not returned. The brother,

* See Note (c), page 22.

"being a single man and a little better off, he thinks as my place ain't quite good enough for him." Expenses are scarcely ever incurred for recreation, but last Bank-holiday they all went for a country walk towards Dulwich, and hired a mail cart for the children, three hours at 1d. an hour. The man himself has never been into a Museum, although born in London. He is sensitive to the feeling that, in any public building, he or his children might be looked down upon as having "no right to be there" because they are not smartly dressed. Neither he nor his wife has been to a theatre or entertainment since marriage. "We have pantomine enough at home," they say. The children play with each other, and with the neighbour's children in the street. They have never been on a steamboat, taken part in an excursion, nor visited any place of special interest.

NOTES.

(*a*) When London workmen are spoken to on the unwisdom of marrying before due provision is made to avoid distress, they not unusually reply that they are led into precipitate marriage owing to the discomfort and swindling experienced in lodgings. It is worthy of consideration whether the economies of community might not be utilized to combine for unmarried workmen some of the comforts of a well managed home with some of the advantages of club life. Compare what is (with special advantages, no doubt) done at the Students' Residences at Wadham House, and Balliol House, close by Toynbee Hall, for the class from which junior clerks are drawn.

(*b*) The superstitious extravagance of the poor in funeral expenses is well known. One of the attractions of the Salvation Army is said to be the quasi-military funeral promised to those who enlist. A brother of this plumber's wife quarrelled with his mother and went to Australia, where he succeeded well. Learning of his mother's illness, he sent home £30 to a comrade, to be applied only to funeral expenses in case of death, and refusing personal correspondence. £16 of the £30 was laid out in the event.

(*c*) On the abolition of school fees the family ceased to trouble to send early to the baker's for cheap stale bread (page 21). See further details of this family in the Royal Statistical Society's Journal, June, 1893, page 284.

2.

[LONDON.]   1892.

Painter, age 51.   *Children : Girls (adopted), ages 14 and 8.*
Wife   age 34.

Budget 2, is that of a house-painter, his wife, and two adopted children. As the period under inquiry is winter, the husband has had no regular employment, while an accident to his hand which he crushed in the cog-wheel of the mangle has been in the way of occasional work. The household has, therefore, been wholly dependent, except for a loan of 2s. 6d. and £1 10s. received as payment of a debt, on the profits of a mangling business taken up by the wife when the husband's work began to fail. The mangle half fills the little kitchen, while the parlour and the passage from the front door are often blocked with bundles of clothes.

The house is in East London; there are four rooms with a kitchen, built out into the yard, and a small scullery beyond; the upper floor, usually sub-let for 5s. or 6s. a week, is so much out of repair that the full house rent of 11s. has been reduced to 5s. 3d. A pair of bantam fowls is kept in the yard.

The husband lived a very unsettled life before marriage. As a boy he tried several trades, and then ran away to sea. He served in the American navy during the war, was, at one time, at the diggings, at another, an overseer in a West Indian plantation. He went, at least, one voyage after marriage, when his wife returned to her trade as dressmaker. He finally settled down as a painter and made a comfortable livelihood till lately.

3.

[LONDON.]   1892.

Painter's Labourer
Wife } *married 27 years.*   Children : *Boys, ages 16 and 14.*

Budget 3, is that of a painter's labourer in London. He has been married 27 years and has a son of 26, and a daughter of 21, living away from home. The two boys at home are shop assistants; they give their entire wages, 12s. a week between them, to the household. The mother earns 3s. a week by charing. The husband has been six years at his present occupation and with his present employer. During this time, he has been seven weeks without work one year, and two or three weeks without it other years. He is paid 6d. an hour, and works 52½ hours in the week, except from November to March, when the hours are 47½. He provides his own aprons, blouses, and knives, at a cost of 10s. a year.

They live in two rooms and have no garden or yard.

4.

[LONDON.]   1891.

[BY THE HEAD OF THE FAMILY.]

Assistant-Relieving Officer, age 26.   Children : *Boys, ages 3, and 2 weeks.*
Wife   *age 27.*   *Girl, age 1.*
Mother   *age 64.*

" At the time of my birth my father was 42 years of age, and was working as a warehouseman in a large firm of house furnishers. He had served an apprenticeship to cabinet-making, but, through failing sight, had abandoned his trade.

" Between the ages of 4 and 5, I was sent to school (a voluntary Church School) and I have a lively recollection of the loving care and attention I received, both in the infants' division and upper classes, the head master at the present time being one of my best friends. At the age of 8 years, having a good treble voice, I joined the church choir, and received from 7s. to 16s. per quarter for my services, a welcome addition to the family income.

" Shortly after my 12th birthday, my father was attacked by a cancer in the tongue and was compelled to give up work. He was a member of a Friendly Society which brought in 10s. per week. My mother had some time previously obtained the care of some offices, earning about 10s. per week, and my sister, four years older than myself, was apprenticed to the pianoforte silking, and was earning a few shillings and partial food. I had, beside, a brother, four years younger, going to school.

" Father continuing to get worse, I was taken away from school, having passed the seventh standard examination, and put to work in his old firm, being promised a junior clerkship, a promise which was never kept ; and I continued to do the work of a furniture porter, which was very distasteful to me. My wages were 6s. per week.

" After one year of this, I applied for a berth in the Railway Clearing House and passed the examination, but, having no influence, I did not obtain work.

" My father died after being at home, ill, for twelve months, I being 14 years of age, and then the struggle for existence began, but we never asked or received charity of any description, and always managed to dress well and live in respectable houses. My mother, at this time, worked very hard and lived harder. This continued until I was nearly 17, when, owing to a quarrel with one of the men, a drunkard, I refused to work with him and was fined 2s. 6d. for insubordination, refused to pay it and left as an alternative.

" I now applied again to the Clearing House, passed two more examinations, and, being recommended by the chairman of one of the London Railways, obtained employment at £35 per annum, rising £10 each year up to £75. About this time I became acquainted with my wife, who was the sister of a shopmate, and was a linendraper's assistant.

" I had also joined the volunteers and served three years, going to the reviews at Brighton, and Portsmouth, my first real holidays, having never before been for more than the annual school excursion, and I would like to say, for the satisfaction of those who subscribe to these treats for children, that it was always the happiest day of the year to me.

" The next four years were very pleasant, although the hard work and the unfamiliar nature of it tried my sight and health very much, but I liked it, and appreciated the Library and Magazine clubs, also the swimming club, of which I was a member of the committee, and then I had my sweetheart and her friends to visit ; altogether, I was very happy. At the end of the four years, I was a successful candidate for my present appointment at £80 per annum, and left home, having to reside in my district. At the end of six months I got married owing to the discomfort of my lodgings, and the effect of the bad living, long hours, standing in close, hot, unhealthy shops on my sweetheart's health.

" I may say, that, with one or two exceptions, my remarks about the bad and insufficient food and the long hours, coupled with the petty tyranny of the shopwalkers and the bad moral effect of men and women working all day long (frequently 16 hours, never less than 12) in the same shop, are universally true and make the drapery trade about the worst a girl can enter. The pay is, however, usually high. Twelve months after marriage I was shifted to another district, and was provided with house accommodation, coals and gas, in addition to my £80. One week after moving my wife was confined, the baby dying through an accident at birth; the nurse got drunk and I had to turn her out, my wife was very ill and had to go to the seaside as soon as she was able. This same week my mother was, also, taken ill and was bedridden twelve months, and has never been able to support herself since. At this time I got into debt about £20 and it has hung like a mill-stone round my neck since, with the interest of 10°/₀ to 15°/₀. When my mother was able to get about, we took a room for her, and my brother and I allowed her 3s. 6d. per week each. This lasted for about one year, when she gave up her room and came to live with me, my brother allowing me 2s. per week ; this lasted till he got married, when he discontinued his allowance, and now she has been wholly dependent on me over twelve months.

" We have now three children, but they are very healthy and so are we. My wife plays the piano and sings very well, and I the violin, a little. I am also a member of the church choir. We have a good many friends to visit, and who visit us, and we go to theatres and concerts as often as we can afford it, or get free passes, and when we are at home alone, we amuse ourselves with music and reading, I still being a member of the Clearing House Literary Societies.

" Two years ago my salary was increased to £90 per annum, and we are gradually recovering from the expenses and losses of our early married life."

5.

[LONDON.]

[BY THE HEAD OF THE FAMILY.]

Dispenser, age 44. *Children : Boy, age* 8.
Wife   *age* 39. *Girls, ages* 10, 6, *and* 2.

" **History of the Family.**—The husband's parents were born in London. His home was till 4 years old in East London. His father sold his business, when the mania for going to America was at its height, 1852. ('To the West, to the West, to the land of the Free &c.') Arrived at Liverpool, he was persuaded to leave his family and go to New York and establish himself, then send for family ; this he did, and after two years returned, like ' Martin Chuzzelwit,' minus his capital.

" He then engaged with a commissariat company to go to the Crimea (Russian War) to feed the English soldiers ; this turned out more profitable than the American expedition. The war being over, he returned and went again to New York with the same result as before.

" Returned to Liverpool, he tried refreshment house keeping, until the American War broke out. He then went to the Southern States and tried blockade-running, with some measure of success, the first time ; the second time the ship sank and he was drowned.

" His mother then boarded the three children out at Liverpool, and went as a nurse and companion to a lady at Southport. Their kind foster parents then (after a few weeks at school) sent them to a factory and bribed them not to tell their mother ; this went on for some time till a friend took his sister, another took his brother, and another took him.

" His new foster parent was a chemist and druggist, who made him an apprentice, making a great sacrifice on his account. Like ' Old Squeers,' he said he would teach him all the mysteries of his business for nothing, for which under ordinary circumstances he charged £200.

" He was 13 years old then, and was with him eight years, and had nothing but drudgery the whole of the time. He had to open shop at 7.30 a.m., and keep in it till 11 p.m. No time for reading or study, and he expects he would have been there still, had not one of his assistants persuaded him to leave and try another situation. This he did, his master upbraiding him for his ingratitude like ' Poor Tom Pinch.' Like a freed slave, he did not know what to do, and would have begged his employer to forgive him and take him back, had not the assistant come to his aid and encouraged him to leave. He then took a junior assistantship with a chemist at Crewe. This was a great improvement ; shorter hours 8 a.m. till 9 p.m. He managed to get to the Crewe Literary Institute from 9 till 10 p.m. occasionally, got some books to read and began to study for the pharmaceutical examination. Rising at 6 a.m. with two other assistants in the town, they got together and worked hard for two years, as he found the £200 premium so generously sacrificed by his master had not done much for him in the way of education.

" He would here pay a tribute of gratitude to the L. & N. W. Railway Company's Literary Institute at Crewe. Had it not been for its reading room and free library, he does not know what he would have done for the necessary books, &c., also for the classes in chemistry, physiology, &c. Free libraries are a boon that should exist everywhere.

" He came to London in 1872 and passed the examination, took a situation in the City, where he stayed on a progressive salary four years. Having saved £100, he bought a partnership in a business at Islington. As there was not enough for both himself and partner to do, he went out as *locum tenens ;* this lasted two years, finding long hours and poor pay not conducive to his health—8 a.m. till 10 p.m., Sundays 6 till 10 p.m. Total receipts £16 a week. After paying expenses there was very little to divide, so he sold his share and took a dispenser's place ; hours 9 a m. till 6 p.m., and finds himself better off every way.

" He has been in this situation 15 years and does not wish to leave it unless he can find a nice business in the country. In London the competition is too great, medicines are made up by Drapers' Stores, &c., so that few who keep open Chemists' Shops make more than a bare living, except those who sell quack medicines to simpletons who are easily pursuaded to buy them, and this he strongly objects to, as he looks upon it as a form of robbery that should be suppressed.

"The wife's father was born in Basingstoke, her mother in London.

"The wife is banker and makes best use of the money, and they manage to live very comfortably; have had nothing to complain about since marriage.

"**Moral Circumstances.**—The children are taught to fear God and honour the Quéen and all in authority under her, to love their neighbours as themselves, and to obey their parents in all things. They all attend the Board School because there is no school so good near enough to send them to; they make good progress, never miss unless through illness.

"Father non-smoker; both take stout with dinner and supper; attend a meeting of Christians twice on Sunday, when possible.

"**Hygiene.**—Husband, wife and children all of good constitution, had very little illness except influenza and complaints common to children. The one five years old fell into the fire-place on Christmas-day, 1891, and was very badly scalded through a pan of water falling on her. This caused an increase in expenditure for beef-tea, chicken-broth, &c., but no expense for medical advice, or medicine; living at the Dispensary all that is free. This is an advantage. There is also the disadvantage of living where there are so many sick daily, as there is great risk of contagion. We frequently find cases of scarlet fever among the patients and other like diseases, although every precaution is taken to prevent their spreading.

"The children play in the public gardens close by, as there is no yard or garden at home.

II.

"The husband is engaged from 9 a.m. till 6 p.m. daily; Saturdays, 9 a.m. till 3 p.m., at the dispensary; and occasionally does a little work after dispensary hours for the doctors, at 1s. per hour.

"The wife does all the house work with the assistance of a charwoman once a week; she also makes and mends all the clothing for herself and the children.

"The children are taught to be useful so far as their age permits; the eldest girl minds the baby, and the others are allowed to play between school hours.

III.

"**Meals.**—Breakfast 8.0 a.m. Cocoa, bread and butter with fish, or eggs and bacon. Bread and milk for children.

"Dinner 1 p.m. Meat with two vegetables. Milk or suet pudding, pancakes or any seasonable fruit stewed. Beer.

"Tea 5 p.m. Tea, bread and butter; children milk and water instead of tea. The children have jam, syrup, or butter, as they like.

"Supper 9.30 p.m. Fish, bread and beer.

" House, coals and gas are supplied free; the house is situated in London, in a very populous district mostly of poor people.

" The family occupies the 2nd and 3rd floors (the rest of the house being used for business purposes).

"Its four rooms are well lighted and ventilated, the front rooms looking upon an open space.

" The 2nd floor is used as kitchen and sitting room, the 3rd as bed rooms. Two girls sleep in the back room, husband, wife, boy and baby in front, which is 15 feet square by 6 feet high. They are not attached to the neighbourhood, the neighbours being very poor and many of them dirty.

" They are frequently disturbed by drunken fights, and rows in the night after the public houses close. The children are often set upon and robbed on their way to and from school.

" Their last residence was in the suburbs in a very quiet corner. The wife feels the change very much, and hopes they will not be long in the same house; after nine years' residence, the vicinity is very cheerless and depressing.

" There is a constant water supply and every convenience, but no yard or garden.

" The furniture and clothing are all that can be desired by persons in their circumstances; everything is as clean and sweet as the smoky neighbourhood will permit.

" **Recreations.**—The husband, wife and children are fond of home, where they are mostly to be found.

" The eldest girl plays the piano, the wife used to, but domestic matters, sewing, mending, &c., will not permit of it now. The children are out, when fine, till six p.m. in the Summer, playing in the public gardens; they go to bed at 7.30 p.m. and get up at 7 a.m.

" The husband goes to the Library and Reading Room, or to assist one of the doctors for an hour or two. Saturday afternoon a trip to Gospel Oak, Hampstead, the Parks or a Museum.

" Have a fortnight at the sea-side in the Summer, which is very much appreciated.

APPENDIX.

" **Thrift.**—The money saved (£230) has been invested in three Building Societies.

" On withdrawing from the first, 50 per cent. was charged for depreciation of property in the hands of the Society, this was a loss of £65.

" The second gave no interest.

" The third became insolvent and although notice of withdrawal was given five years ago, nothing has been received from it as yet.

" The Post Office Savings Bank is now the receiver of their quarterly balance, and is safe, sure and reliable."

6.

Soapboiler,   *age* 41.   *Children : Girls, ages* 12 *and* 10.
Wife   *age* 40.
Female boarder, age 34.

Budget 6 is that of a vegetarian family. The husband is a soap-boiler in London. He was born near the Strand, was left an orphan at sixteen, and then lived with a grandmother, whom he helped to keep. He was at that time in the retail shop of a small firm of soap-boilers. He is still with the same firm, but was long ago transferred to the factory at Finsbury.

He has been married fourteen years. His wife was a domestic servant, the daughter of a recruiting-sergeant, who died when she was two years old. Besides the two children, there is another member of the household—the head mistress of a small infants' school, who has boarded with them nearly two years. She pays 6s. for board, and 5s. 6d. for two unfurnished rooms for her mother and herself. The mother provides her own board, independently of the rest of the household.

The husband's special work is the perfuming of scented soaps. The ordinary wages for his post are 30s. ; he receives 35s. because of his long service. The hours are from 8 a.m. to 6.30 p.m., with one hour for dinner and half-an-hour for tea. On Saturdays he goes on till two o'clock with no intervals. He takes his dinner and bread and butter for tea from home, but buys his own tea from the 2s. a week he reserves for his private purse.

They live in a seven-roomed house in a pleasant and airy situation. The furniture is rather scanty, and all the rooms are not used. On the boarder's recommendation, they have adopted Dr. Allinson's system of diet, and live chiefly on wholemeal flour and fruit ; these appear in some form at every meal. They also use vegetables, eggs, butter, porridge, tea, and fish occasionally. Only the husband eats meat. For recreation, he reads a few newspapers, such as the *Echo* and *Tit-Bits*, the *Strand Magazine*, and a Sunday weekly. He takes long walks on Saturdays and Sundays. A recent visit of six days to the home of his mother-in-law near Southampton is the longest holiday he has ever had. His wife and children stayed a month, incurring no expense except for travelling and 4s. a week for one bedroom out.

Their savings are small. Before the last two years they had acted as caretakers to unlet houses in various parts of London for seven years. Now that they have incurred the additional expense of house-rent, they find it difficult to keep their expenditure much below their income.

7.

Journeyman Slipper-maker, age 38.   *Children : Boys, ages* 11, 10, 6 *and* 1.
Wife   *age* 37.   *Girls, ages* 8 *and* 4.

Budget 7 is that of a Jewish family. The husband is a journeyman slipper-maker, born in Germany and taken to England when six months old.   He was brought up in Manchester, but has been many years in London.   He has been married twelve years. His wife's father was foreign, her mother English.   The husband has been twenty-five years at his trade, and eight years with his present employer.   He works eighty to eighty-four hours a week, thirteen or fourteen hours a day not being considered long at his trade.   He finds his own grindery :—hemp, wax, cardboard, paste, sand-paper, nails, emery cloth, etc., estimated to cost 5d. for each dozen pairs of slippers made.   Prices for making range from 3½d. to 5¼d. per pair, and are declining.   When without work, he buys his own material (funds allowing) and makes to sell in the open market.   Materials thus bought make up a good part of "expenses of industry."   The wife makes 2s. 6d. a week by slipper-binding at home.

The food is bought from a small general-shop in the neighbourhood.   High prices are knowingly paid for some articles for the sake of the convenience of getting credit in hard times.   They live in a four-roomed cottage in East London.   See further details of this family in the Royal Statistical Society's Journal, June, 1893, page 283.

8.

[LONDON.]   1892.

Widow.   *Children : Sons, ages 19, [13] and 9.*
Two Servants.   *Daughters, ages 23, 21, 17 and 15.*

This family, whose budget (No. 8) is given for one year, is in good circumstances, the mother, a widow, having a private income of £715 a year.

The eldest son is in business.   Of the four daughters, the eldest teaches ; the second has just left college ; the two younger girls and two boys are at school, the elder of the two boys at a boarding-school.   The eldest son and daughter have small salaries, out of which they pay personal expenses, such as clothes, travelling, and dinners away from home ; the daughter also contributes £15 a year towards household expenses.

The house is in a suburb of London ; the rent is £90, or, including taxes, water rate and garden expenses, just over £120.

So far as can be gathered from the budget and short monograph, the family is a typical one of the well-to-do middle class ; two servants are kept ; the early dinner is supplemented by a meat or fish supper.   The yearly summer holiday and occasional "outings" form the main recreations.

In tabulating the budget, many of the items could not be separated to fit the various divisions framed with special reference to the budgets of working-men ; thus butter, fats, bacon, cheese, were included under "cheesemonger;" milk and eggs under "milkman."   The stationers' bill, covering paper, stamps, newspapers, magazines, was tabulated under "other expenses."

PROVINCIAL TOWNS.

9.

[LIVERPOOL]   1891.

[BY THE COMPILER. FICTITIOUS NAMES HAVE BEEN USED.]

Carpenter, age 65.   *Lodgers (see text.)*
Wife   age 50.

Mr. and Mrs. Walker live in a six-roomed house in Turner Street, Liverpool. Mrs. Walker is an active woman of about 50. Her husband is much older, possibly 65. They have no family, the only child of the marriage having died shortly after birth.

Walker is by trade a carpenter, and has been accustomed to regular wages in connection with the care of property. He was formerly, and for a long time, connected with the office of Lord D——'s agent but on the death of the latter, lost his place. His wife was waitress at a restaurant before marriage, and while her husband was out of work earned money as a cleaner at the Municipal offices. After a considerable period out of work, Walker obtained employment from a rather skin-flint owner of small property, who now only pays him 15s. a week in summer and 12s. in winter. With this Walker has to be satisfied, if not content, as he is too old and possibly too little skilled to obtain work at trade prices. His wife makes up the income by taking lodgers and letting off some of the rooms. The house is well situated for this purpose. It is very central with a south aspect, and stands on the brow of rather a steep hill, in a fairly wide street. Great thoroughfares, along which the tram cars run, lie on every side, but through Turner street itself the traffic is for the most part on foot, and the street has become a children's playground. The upper part of this street is dignified on the one side by the district church, and on the other by a Quaker meeting house ; at the back of the Walker's house is situated a diminutive " square " which, if it were less respectable, would be called a " court." Immediately round about there is a net-work of courts and narrow streets, many of them of the poorest kind, and all swarming with inhabitants. Among these there is a colony of Italian organ-grinders, who may be heard in the morning tuning and trying their instruments, and changing or putting in order the pegged barrels which constitute the mechanism of the tunes they play.

Sources of Income are :—

(1) WAGES at 15s. up to November, and afterwards at 12s., except that in one week only 7s. is acknowledged to have been received. The 5s. was, I believe, nevertheless received, and should appear as " pocket money " for Mr. W., or be added to the money " not accounted for." As a rule, Mr. W. gives all his wages to his wife, who buys his tobacco and gives him money for

shaving. He also takes an occasional shilling for the public-house., If he is treated by a lodger, he must return the compliment at times.

(2) LETTING OF ROOMS, &c. Shortly before the account begins things had gone astray, and at first none of the rooms were well let. The parties occupying the first floor front, a painter and his wife, were unsatisfactory. The woman had a disreputable appearance. Mrs. Walker said she could not do with the woman standing in the door with a shawl over her head. So they left, and after being unoccupied for several weeks, the room was taken by Mr. and Mrs. Park, with one little girl. Park was employed on•the construction of the Dockside Railway. Both he and his wife drank a good deal, but they paid their rent regularly. In the parlour (ground floor) there was a sailor and his wife. He went to sea and she left, and the room was taken by Mr. and Mrs. Wheatley. W. was a clown, and was mostly away with some circus. His wife, who had charge of some performing dogs, finally left in the seventeenth week because the Walkers objected to a sick dog sharing her room. It was then taken by Mr. and Mrs. Hill at 6s. a week. Hill was nominally a cabinet maker, and she "such a lady-like looking woman." They were people who always "expected money" which seldom came. They left at last, £2 8s. 6d. in debt to the Walkers. The back room on the first floor was unfurnished but was taken for a few nights by an American who did without a bed. An old debt paid in the fourth week provided funds to complete the equipment, and the room was then let furnished, first to a sick artist, who paid 4s. 6d. with attendance, and afterwards to a married couple at 4s. without attendance. These three rooms brought in, in all, £11 15s. 6d. in the twenty-two weeks.

The front cellar is let to an advertising agent, at 1s. 3d. a week, as a store for "sandwich" boards. The back part of the cellar beneath the kitchen is used for the Walkers' coals. The front room on the second floor holds two beds, and accommodates two, three, or at times four men, who are charged 3s. 6d. a week, or 1s. for a single night ; no less than £6 14s. came in from this source of income. Three weeks yielded the full 14s., five weeks 10s. 6d. or 11s., and the other weeks smaller sums or nothing. The married occupants of the separate rooms find their own food and expect no service, beyond what arises from friendly consideration ; but the men usually take their suppers in the kitchen and sit there in the evening, and Mrs. Walker cooks and washes for them. The charges made for what they have are very moderate, but, still, leave a small margin on the money actually laid out, this being very well earned by the work done by Mrs. Walker.* The bills amount in total to about £10, of which more than half fell in the eleventh, twelfth and thirteenth weeks, when the house was filled with stage carpenters and scene-shifters belonging to two London theatrical companies successively visiting Liverpool. But towards the end of the time the room became regularly occupied by three artisans, who are the most desirable tenants, as being most regular and permanent.

---

*Mrs. Walker charges 9d. for Sunday dinner, about 6d. for a meat tea, and 3d. or 4d. for breakfast or tea with fish or egg.

(3) LOANS RETURNED.—A first item, 6s. 4d., is the landlord's proportion of taxes paid in a previous week and recovered from him. A second item, £1 9s., represents the payment of a debt of long standing, being six weeks rent of the parlour at 5s. The tenants left with this in arrears, and Mrs. Walker held some pawn tickets as security. The debtor received money from a son settled in Australia for a passage out, and used part to redeem his watch, &c. One shilling was spent to secure the 29s., which had been almost despaired of. The remaining amounts, £1 2s. 5d. in all, were sums repaid by lodgers or neighbours, against £1 10s. 6d. lent, from which it appears that 7s. 11d. was due at the end, but it may be that part of this had been collected and forgotten.

The smallest total income in any week was £1 and the largest £4 14s. 4d. The smallest amount spent was £1 1s. and the largest £3 3s. 8½d. Amid such irregularities it is useless to talk of averages, but on the whole, in twenty-two weeks £47 12s 7d. was received and £41 10s. 11d. was spent, or £42 9s. 1d., if we include money not accounted for, the final result being savings in hand of £5 3s. 6d.

There were ten weeks* in which only 10s 1d. altogether was charged to lodgers for supplies. In these ten weeks 112s. 1½d. was spent for food,† Deducting the 10s. 1d., we have an average cost of maintenance for Mr. and Mrs. Walker of a little over 10s. a week. The whole average expenditure of 11s. 2½ per week may be divided as follows :—cereals, 1s. 2½d., fats, 1s. 7½d., milk, &c., 1s. 1½d., meat, &c., 2s. 9d., vegetables, 1s. 3½d., sugar, 9d., drinks, 2s. 1½d., cat and bird, 4d.=11s. 2½d. The 10s. 1d. received from lodgers would probably be represented by a slight increase in the meat and vegetable bill connected with Sunday dinner.

Mr. Walker begins work at six o'clock, and may sometimes return for breakfast or dinner, or both, but more generally he carries breakfast and dinner "cut up," together with two small packets of tea mixed with sugar which, infused in boiling water, make his beverage. Slices of bread and butter are supplied for breakfast, and of bread and meat for dinner, with sometimes a piece of pie or cake. He comes home to tea and eats again bread and butter, with occasionally an egg or a little fish, but more commonly some pudding or a piece of pie. Mrs. Walker is a very fair cook. She herself has usually a slice of bacon or an egg for breakfast and takes tea with her husband. I do not know what she does for dinner, probably nothing very set. They have coffee at 9 or 9.30, with a biscuit or bread and cheese or slice of cake or remains of a cold pudding.

The habits of the lodgers vary very much. For some Mrs. Walker "cuts up" meals, as for her husband ; some get all their meals out ; most commonly, they have tea or supper at home. They may eat bread and butter with a haddock or a herring or an egg, or have a good supply of meat and potatoes, but they usually drink tea. Some share the evening coffee, and some drink beer at bed time. The stage carpenters and scene shifters had a very solid late breakfast, and looked for a hot supper at midnight, when their work was done.

---

*The 22nd week is not included as it contained only six days, and no Saturday—Saturday being 1st January.

†The sum of 2s. 5½d. was not accounted for in these weeks, and may have been (all or part) spent on food

Expenditure :—

An analysis of the expenditure will throw some further light on the habits and conditions of life in this household. Provisions are bought at shops in the immediate neighbourhood.

CEREALS—As much is spent on flour as on bread. Mrs. Walker bakes every week, unless she is very busy, as was especially the case in the tenth, eleventh and twelfth weeks, when the theatrical men were lodging with her. She makes excellent bread. Baker's bread, when she buys it, consists of the best small loaves costing about 1½d. a lb. The rice is used for puddings. She also makes a bread pudding of the scraps once a week. Flour is 8-lbs. for 1s. ; rice 2d. per lb.

FATS.—About equal amounts are spent on butter and on bacon. Mrs. Walker pays: butter 1s. or margarine 8d., bacon 6d., dripping 4d., and lard 6d. per lb. She uses lard for frying and dripping for pastry, of which Mr. Walker is very fond.

MILK is used with tea and coffee three times a day, and the cat always has his share. It is also used for the rice puddings. On the whole nearly as much is spent on milk as on butter. The price is 3d. per quart. Mr. W. takes buttermilk sometimes. Eggs are mostly used for the lodgers. The cheese costs 6d. per lb.

MEAT costs 6d. or 6½d, with occasionally a bit of steak at 8d. per lb. Haddock and herring are the fish used, and price varies with the size.

VEGETABLES—Potatoes cost 9d. or 10d. per peck (20 lbs.) ; other vegetables and fruit include a considerable variety, according to the season.

SUGAR costs 2d. per lb., white-crystallized or loaf only being used.

TEA costs 1s. 10d., or 2s. for "ticket tea," and 1s. 4d. for cheap tea, where no "tickets" are given (tickets are a discount). It may be noticed that tea, milk, butter and bacon all account for about the same sum.

COFFEE costs 1s. per lb., and a quarter-of-a-pound is the regular weekly allowance for themselves.

BEER, &c., charged is all for lodgers. When Mr. W. has a glass he goes out for it, and the cost comes out of pocket-money.

TOBACCO costs 1½d. per oz., and half-an-ounce is Mr. W.'s usual daily consumption.

MEDICINE was for Mr. Walker's rheumatism. He got better gradually.

PETS—The old cat—a singular character and great favourite—died the week before Christmas. He slept on his mistress's pillow, and would sit on the table beside her at tea time, and help himself to milk by dipping his paw in the jug. He never left the house. On one occasion, venturing into the street he was lost, and after many days was found, exhausted with hunger, in the cellar of the adjoining house, into which, by some mistake, he had found his way. The birds were two linnets, whose cages hung by the kitchen window.

RENT began a week in arrears, and this back week was made up gradually from the twelfth to the sixteenth week—thus twenty-three weeks are included in the account. The poor rate, &c.,

£1 5s. 4d., is for twelve months. Taxes, £3 18s., had been paid before this account begins, and of this 6s. 4d., the landlord's tax, appears as a receipt in the first week of the account. On the whole the true share of rates and taxes for twenty-two weeks would be £2 1s. 1d., whereas only 19s. was paid out on this account; this disposes of £1 3s. of the apparent surplus. The landlord appears to be a just man, ready to do what repairs and decorations are needed from time to time.

FUEL—Coals were 10d. per cwt. Chips are usually home-made as Mr. Walker has opportunities of getting old wood.

LIGHT used is petroleum, costing 2d. a quart. Bed room candles are sometimes used.

FURNITURE, besides bed and bedding bought for the back room, consists of a general plenishing ; rather more may have been spent than would ordinarily be necessary to maintain the house. The principal items are : Bed stocks, palliasse and bed, 10s. 6d. ; sheets 1s. 7d., 3s. 6d., 1s. 3d.; towels 1s. 6d. ; kettle 1s. ; mending clock 1s. 6d. ; recovering stolen clock 1s. 6d. ; and another iron bedstead 4s. : this was to replace an old wooden half-tester, broken up because infested with bugs ; constant war has to be waged in this direction.

WASHING.—Mrs. Walker washes for the house, including lodgers' clothes—a service which is included in the charge of 3s. 6d. a week—but gives out collars, cuffs, &c., to the laundry, charging the cost in the men's weekly bills. She pays for mangling of the household linen, &c. The £1 6s. 4d. expended is thus made up of cost of washing materials, and payments to laundry and mangle. Laundry charges: Collars, 1d. ; fronts, 1½d. ; cuffs, 2d. ; shirts, 4d. Mangling is a 1d. and wringing 1d. per dozen.

SERVICE is for the assistance of a woman on washing days, when Mrs. Walker is busy.

CLOTHING is mainly for herself, but includes whatever Mr. Walker spends—chiefly on boots.

POCKET MONEY includes shaving, and pays for an occasional evening at the "Castle." Mr. Walker takes no other amusement, and brings all his wages home ; except that, as already stated, one week he seems to have kept 5s. for some purpose not explained.

CLUB is really an insurance in the Prudential ; 6d. per week for Mr. Walker, begun 11 years ago when he was accepted as 50, gives £18 at death; and 3d. a week for his wife, begun at same time, she being 38, gives £14 at death.

LENT—This account requires some further explanation. Money paid out on account of lodgers explains part ; the tenants occasionally borrow small sums, and, finally, a running account appears to have been kept with two intimate neighbours. Mrs. Walker is always the lender, and it may be supposed that to have cash in hand is the exception amongst the residents in Turner Street.

It may be of interest to consider the value to be found in the business of letting lodgings, as shown by the accounts.

To make the figures complete it is necessary to include in the receipts 4s. a week for the second floor back room, which Mr. and

Mrs. Walker slept in. This is the rent they charge for it when they occupy another room themselves. Twenty-two weeks at 4s. would be £4 8s. If they lived elsewhere they would have to pay at least as much as this. We then have for twenty-two weeks:

	Cellar produced for 22 weeks	£1	8	0
	Parlour	4	2	0
	Front room 1st floor	4	2	6
	Back ,, ,, ...	3	11	0
RECEIPTS	Lodgers in top room	6	14	0
	Mr. & Mrs. Walker, for use of top back room	4	8	0
	Lodgers' bills for food and washing	9	16	4

TOTAL £34 1s. 10d.

	Rent for 22 weeks	£9	5	2
	Proportion of Rates & Taxes	2	1	0
	Fire and light..	2	8	0
	Furniture..	2	7	0
	Washing and hired service ..	1	11	0
EXPENDITURE.	Cost of lodgers' food £19 8s. 7d. less £12 2s. 0d., taking the Walker's own expenditure for food and washing of clothes at 11s. per week ..	7	6	7
	Expended and not accounted for	0	18	2

TOTAL £25 16s. 11d.

This shows a profit margin of £8 4s. 11d. or 7s. 6d. per week earned by Mrs. Walker—the rooms bringing in 22s. per week against 29s. 9d. per week if fully occupied, or an allowance for failure in letting of 25%.

The account of Mr. and Mrs. Walker would then stand thus :—

RECEIPTS	Mr. Walker's wages for 22 weeks, (adding the 5s. omitted)	£15	6	0
	Mrs. Walker's earnings ...	8	4	11

TOTAL £23 10s. 11d.

	Food, &c., for 22 weeks ..	£12	2	0
	Clothing..	1	18	6
EXPENDITURE.	Pocket money—Mr. Walker (adding the 5s.)..	0	16	11
	Insurance ., ...	0	16	6
	Rent	4	8	0

TOTAL £20 1s. 11d.

Showing a margin of £3 9s. 0d.*

It must not be forgotten that Mrs. Walker's earnings require the possession of capital in the form of furniture. On the other hand, the money spent on furniture in these twenty-two weeks would probably suffice to meet depreciation as well as renewal and interest. Depreciation as well as renewal must be provided, because in case of sale, or even removal, there is a heavy loss on furniture. Mrs. Walker informs me that when she came into the house six years ago, she spent about £15, buying what she required at the auction rooms. Assuming, however, that £20 would be needed at the outset, and taking ten per cent. depreciation and five per cent. interest, and another ten per cent. for renewals, we should require £5 per annum, whereas an expenditure of £2 7s. for twenty-two weeks is equal to £5 11s. per annum.

* This margin of £3 9s. can be compared with that of £5 3s. 6d. shown in the actual account by adding 29s. old debt collected, and 21s. proportion of rates and taxes not paid, making £5 19s., and deducting one week's extra rent, 8s. 5d., and 7s. 11d., apparently due for loans, making £5 2s. 8d. (error 10d).

An inventory of the furniture will complete this story.

Top front room.

2 full size beds complete
1 dressing table and looking glass
1 washstand and crockery service
4 chairs.
Carpet and fender
Muslin curtains and roller blind
Recess cupboard (fixture)

Top back room.

1 full size bed complete
1 dressing table and looking glass
1 washstand and crockery
2 chairs
2 pairs of curtains for windows
(no fireplace)

1st floor front room.

1 full size bed complete
1 centre table and cloth
1 large chest of drawers
1 dressing table and looking glass
1 washstand and crockery
3 chairs
Oil cloth and strips of carpet
Fender
Muslin curtains and roller blind
2 recess cupboards—fixtures
Chimney ornament and 8 or 10 pictures

1st floor back room.

1 single bed complete
1 dressing table and looking glass
1 chair
Fender
Hanging bookcase
Picture
Carpet
Window curtains and roller blind

Passage, &c.

Oil cloth, brass rods on stairs
3 mats

Parlour.

1 full size bed complete
1 small table
1 mahogany folding card table
4 chairs
Toilet service on fixture in recess
Fender and fire irons
Mantel glass and small glass on wall
Ornaments and a large number of pictures
Carpet and hearth rug
White curtains and roller blind
Plants in window

Kitchen.

1 sofa
2 tables with oilcloth covers
1 arm chair
1 rocking chair with arms
2 Windsor chairs and 1 stool
Fender and fire stools, &c. (very good)
Cupboard and drawers in recess
Bird cages
Medicine chest (used as desk)
2 work boxes and stand for cotton reels
Oilcloth on floor
2 hearth rugs (1 kept for best)
6 brass candlesticks (bright)
6 dish covers   ,,
2 coffee pots   ,,
2 japanned tea trays ,,
Walls decorated with oleographs

Linen, &c.

19 sheets
12 single and 1 double blankets
7 quilts
Pillow slips, towels
Toilet covers

Scullery.

1 table
1 plate rack

Utensils in Scullery and elsewhere in the house.

3 rolling pins	1 knife board
1 potatoe masher	2 sweeping brushes
1 pastry board	2 hand brushes
1 chopping board	Shoe brushes
2 dutch ovens	2 clothes lines
3 kettles	3 pan mugs
9 pans	9 tumblers
1 fish kettle	5 dishes
5 baking tins (meat)	1 large vegetable
4 cake tins	dish
2 small trays	4 small, ditto
2 strainers	3 pie dishes
1 nutmeg grater	3 sauce boats
1 flour dredger	1 cruet stand
3 candlesticks	1 mustard pot
2 oil cans	3 salt cellars
1 milk can	57 plates (various
1 knife box	kinds)
12 knives	4 jugs
12 forks	25 cups
4 table spoons	28 saucers
2 dessert spoons	5 slop basins
12 tea spoons	4 sugar basins
1 corkscrew	3 butter dishes
1 soup ladle	3 teapots
1 fish slice	1 coffee pot
3 wash bowls	4 milk or cream jugs
1 soap box	7 egg cups
1 comb box and	1 glue pot
comb and brush	2 coal shovels
2 looking glasses	1 coal hammer

Note by Compiler.—In this household I have myself lived a great deal, lodging here a part of every week for months in succession. Altogether I have known the Walkers in this way, pretty intimately, for three years. Mrs. Walker takes a great deal of trouble to make her lodgers comfortable, doing everything for them in a spirit of downright kindness, and Mr. Walker on his part, being a ready riser, gives a call to any who have to begin work early. A home like this, with bed and fireside, cooking, washing, and mending, and an early call if required, to say nothing of pleasant company and kind words, does not seem dear at 6d. a day, and the small profit made out of what is charged to the lodgers for meals well cooked and nicely served, in Mrs. Walker's comfortable kitchen.

The period of the budget was for the Walkers a time of more than usual difficulty and of extra effort. Mrs. Walker is a very hard working, thrifty, and most respectable woman, and as an ordinary thing never takes even a glass of beer, but occasionally this excellent habit breaks down, and when it breaks down it does so very much, and the household goes to pieces. Mr. Walker then stays from work to look after his wife, and first priming and then loading himself with drink (he too, usually, a quiet sober man) his remonstrances grow more and more forcible, both of tongue and fist. I believe these outbreaks have been periodic. I have witnessed two. The last of these in the Spring of 1891 was the worst, and lasted two or three months, on and off. Before it began the Walkers had been doing very well. Their apartments were let, they had respectable lodgers in the spare room, and there was a substantial sum in the savings bank. When the fit was over, the apartments were empty, the lodgers had left, the money was spent and the bank book burnt, the rent was at least a week behind hand, the taxes were due, and Mr. Walker was out of work. After a short drilling of enforced idleness he was reinstated by his employer, but instead of 20s. a week in Summer and 15s. in Winter, which before had been thought little enough, he was offered and dare not refuse, 15s. for Summer and 12s. for Winter.

The Walkers then borrowed £3 18s. to pay the taxes, and bravely set to work to retrieve their position. The budget shows with what success. By Christmas they had reorganized the house and had saved £5. To this they were able to add the 22s. paid for the keeping of these accounts, and so made up a total of £6 2s. to pay £3 18s. owed. Nor has the effort been relaxed, for in spite of losing £2 8s. 6d. by the parlour lodgers in the Spring, they have paid the taxes, and there is now on the 30th August, 1892, £10 10s. in the bank; Mrs. Walker has joined the Good Templars, and all seems well.

10.

[MANCHESTER.]   1893.

Widow, age 66.   *Daughter, age 23.*

Number 10 is the budget of the widow of a German clock-maker, living with her daughter. She was born in Shropshire, and has been a widow four years. She has always been poor, and now her daughter is her sole support. The daughter is a machinist, making fancy aprons in a warehouse. Her income is limited by the amount of work she can get; she never has as much as she can do. They are much more comfortable when they have a lodger, but have been without one for nearly a year. Through agencies at the church and chapel which they attend, the mother gets gifts of clothing and help in illness when she would otherwise be in great difficulties.

11.

[MANCHESTER]. 1893.

Widow. *Son, age 18.*

Budget 11 is that of a widow. The husband was a labourer, and died nine years ago. When her three daughters were at home working, she was comfortably off, but they married young. She has occasional help from one of them, and is otherwise dependent on a son of eighteen, a " hooker" in a warehouse. She has no regular employment, but does charing and caretaking when she can get it.

12.

[ST. IVES, CORNWALL.] 1892.

Railway Labourer. *Sons (2).*
Wife. *Daughters (3).*

Budget 12 is that of a railway labourer born and brought up in St. Ives. He has been married fourteen years, and has been thirteen years at his present occupation. His hours are uncertain, generally eleven-and-a-half hours a day, though sometimes longer. During the period under inquiry he has been engaged in light work because of an accident the previous year. He also had to give up the stable work which he had done for the doctor before and after railway hours. This was taken up by his eldest son for 4s. a week. Since the monograph was drawn up, the man has died, ten days after an epileptic seizure.

The house is a two-roomed cottage with an out-house ; it looks on a stable-yard, and there are stables below the bedroom. The place is unsanitary and dirty. There is no garden.

The accounts have been kept by the eldest son, as the mother cannot write. She is a bad manager, and constantly gets into debt.

13.

[ST. IVES, CORNWALL.] 1893.

Fisherman. *Children : Boys, ages 8, 7 and 4.*
Wife. *Girl, age 5 months.*

The household of budget 13 consists of a fisherman, his wife and four children, two of them step-children. The husband was born in St. Ives, Cornwall, and has always lived there. He has been married five years.

He has been a fisherman for twelve years. He goes out line fishing, on all-night work, working on his own account, but

owning neither net nor boat ; to hire a boat he clubs with three
others.   He has no regular earnings, sometimes making nothing
for weeks, sometimes 8s., 11s., or 14s. per week.   He also does
odd work occasionally, such as boat painting.   The harbour dues,
divided between the four who hire the boat, are 10s. for the
season ; other expenses are 3s. 6d. or 4s. each for lines, and a
share of the catch for the hire of the boat, and for the use of other
men's labour.   One shilling is entered for travelling to and from
work (period not stated), in the note book provided by the
Economic Club, but is not entered in the accounts, nor mentioned
in the monograph.   •

The family lives in a three-roomed cottage, one of a small
double row forming a narrow alley.   They seldom eat meat, and
live chiefly on bread and tea.

The wife cannot read or write ; the accounts were dictated to
the compiler.   She cannot get credit at the shop, but gets a little
help from a sister and from neighbours.

14.

[ASHFORD.]   1891.

Railway Foreman, age 54.   *Children : Sons, ages 18 and 11.*
Wife,   age 52.   *Daughters, ages 13 and 8.*

Budget 14 is that of a foreman in the S.E. Railway Company's service in a town in Kent.   He was born near Hythe.
After leaving school, he worked on his uncle's farm for three
years ; he was for two years a cleaner in the S.E.R. Co.'s factory
for the production of rolling stock ; after a few years in the Militia
he obtained employment in the Goods Department of the Company, and in seven years became foreman.   He has been in the
service of the Company about thirty-four years.   He has been
married thirty-two years.   His wife is a native of Kent, and was
formerly a domestic servant.   Two sons are away from home ;
the eldest, a driver on the S.E.R., is married and living at
Deal ; the second is in the army.   The two elder girls are in
service near London, as parlour-maid and upper housemaid ; they
clothe and help to keep an invalid sister, who is apprenticed to a
dressmaker.*   The third son is a turner in the railway factory ; he
gives a small contribution to the family income, which probably
covers the apparent deficit of 4s. 6½d. a week.

Besides his wages, 24s. a week, the husband has uniform provided by the railway company, and has the right of privilege fares
at ¼d. a mile.   Wages are not withheld during illness.   The hours
are from 6.30 a.m. to 7.30 p.m., with intervals of half-an-hour for
breakfast and one hour for dinner ; these he has at home.   The
work, moving heavy goods, is very exhausting and the warehouse
is draughty.

They live in a healthy four-roomed cottage belonging to the
railway company.   It is fairly well furnished.   There is a garden
attached to the house, and they also hold a strip of land from the

---

* The daughter (20) mentioned in list of family, but not elsewhere, is apparently not at home.

railway company, for growing potatoes, at the nominal rent of 3s. a year. The annual value of both together is about £5, and they obtain from them all the vegetables they need. They use a good deal of meat and milk. They purchase coals, boots, and the greater part of their clothing through clubs; the wife pays 1s. a fortnight to a coal club, 1s. a week to a clothing club, and the husband pays 26s. per quarter for two shares in a shoe club.

The family is delicate, and the doctor's bills are often heavy. A bill of £8 is still unpaid. The husband is far from strong, and has a constant cough.

15.

[SCOTLAND.]   1892.

[BY THE HEAD OF THE FAMILY.]

Artisan.   *Children : ages,* 11, 7, 4 *and* 2.
Wife.

" Family budget written for the purpose of showing how much comfort can be attained and provision made for the contingencies of life, and these are want of work when trade is dull, sickness, old age, and the needs of wife and family in the event of death over-taking the father while the family is young.

" As shown by the family budget given on the other side, it will be seen that for a family of six persons living in comfort and on the best of food (believing that it is best to buy a good thing, and it is always found to be cheapest in the end) that it takes on an average 23s. to provide us with the necessaries of life, giving an average per head of 3s. 10d. per week ; to that has to be added an outlay of 10s. 5d. per week, composed of the following items :—

	£	s.	d.
" Burgh Assessments, which include Poor Rate, School Rate, for Police maintenance, &c., Water Rate, &c., an average per week of ...	0	1	3
Coal	0	1	2
Gas	0	0	7
Benefit Societies	0	1	9
Life Insurance for £100...	0	1	2
Newspapers, &c.	0	0	5
Average for up-keep of clothes, boots, &c. ...	0	2	6
Church purposes	0	1	7
Total	0	10	5
For food	1	3	0
	£1	13	5

" **Income.**—My average income for this year has been about 43s. per week, but when trade is good it will be about 47s. per week, and that leaves me an average balance of about 13s. per week, or £33 16s. per year, out of which I meet my rent. The

average rent of artizans' houses with us is £9 10s. per year, giving
a surplus of £24 6s. per year.   I did not put down my rent
because I have no stated rent ; I can pay as much or as little as I
wish, having built my house through our building society.   I can
pay any sum from £12 10s. yearly, only I have this incentive,
that the more I pay in the form of rent the sooner it will be my
own.   Again I have an average income of from £12 to £14 per
year which I do nothing to earn, and that is the profit on purchases
made in the co-operative society of which we are members and out
of which we purchase all our goods.

" **Societies.**—The benefits I would receive for the 1s. 9d. per
week that I pay are these—if sick I would receive for the first six
months 22s. per week and during illness 10s. per week, with
doctor's attendance and medicine free, also £22 at death.   If I
meet with an accident from which I could not follow my employment I would be able to claim £100 from one society and 5s. per
week from another, and if spared to see old age, that is 60 years,
I will have 10s. per week of superannuation benefit, and 10s. per
week if out of work through dulness of trade.

" **Insurance.**—For the 1s. 2d. per week I am insured for £100
at death, whenever that may happen, so that in all my wife and
children would receive £122 at my decease.

" In the works with which I am connected there is an accident
fund, but it is so little we pay that we never know anything about
it.   By agreement with the workmen our masters keep 3d. per
month of the pay of all men earning £1 per week and upwards,
2d. of all men under £1 per week, and they add an equal amount.
The fund is managed by an equal number of representatives from
masters and men, and gives 15s. per week to first class and 10s. per
week to second class, when off work by accident, be it ever so
slight, so long as the doctor says you are unfit to work ; and when
a fatal accident happens the friends* of the first class receive £40
and the second £30, and all under 11s. pay 1d. per week, and they
receive 5s. per week and £20 if accident proves fatal.

" Doctor's expenses I have not put down any ; the children are
all very healthy and we do not have the doctor very much ; last
year the bill was only 12s.   We had a good deal of doctor's
expenses when first married.

" Table shewing dinners for week beginning Sunday, 31st
January :—

Sunday.—Apple tart and tea.†

Monday.—Soup, meat and potatoes ; ½-lb. boiling meat.

Tuesday.—Stewed meat and vegetables and potatoes ; ¾-lb.
       stewing meat.

Wednesday.—Soup made with bone, and remainder of apple
       tart left from Sunday.

Thursday.—Collops, vegetables and potatoes ; ¾-lb. collops.

Friday.—Soup and semolina pudding.

Saturday.—Stewing meat and potatoes ; ¾-lb. meat.

" Children get no butcher's meat, they get the sauce and
potatoes, and a piece of bread after, and mother and I have always
a cup of coffee after dinner.

---

* Scotch for relatives.
† No meat as a rule, partly to leave the mother leisure for church, &c.

" Sir,— I will give you a short account of what we have done since we were married. In the first ten years we saved past £150, and that after taking all the pleasures of life. We are all well clothed; our house is comfortably furnished (the household goods are insured for £150 in case of fire); every holiday, that is at the fair and new year, during the first eight or nine years of our married life, we were always away from home, we never refrained from enjoying ourselves in a legitimate way, but we always took care to keep it within bounds. I had not always as large an income as I now have, but I remember my wife saved 18s. of her first pay, although there were many things she could have spent it upon, but she has always made her needs subservient to her means. She was not many days married until she began to knit me under-clothing, and from that to this neither my children nor myself has ever worn any under-clothing that has not been made with her own hand; the children's clothes have all been made by her own hands, she having a sewing machine. If there is anything bought at any time, made and ready, it is for the purpose of getting a pattern from for future things.

" To show what can be done I will give an example : there was a sale of goods that had been lying in stock for some time ; my wife bought a piece of strong cloth for 15s., out of which she has made a suit of clothes for church, one pair of trousers for school, for our eldest boy, aged 10 past, a little overcoat for his brother aged 3½ years, and there is as much left as will make an overcoat for some of them in the coming winter if required, that is why I am able to put 2s. 6d. per week down for the upkeep of boots, clothing, etc. She also for the first five or six years made all her own dresses, but gave it up when the children began to need her time.

" I think I have said enough to show how we have saved means while taking the good of life ; we are now reaping the benefits ; we are able to live in our own house at a comparatively early age ; we have a house of five apartments, with bath-room, closet and out-houses, with a piece of garden. My own part in the house-keeping is not much ; I give up into her hands my pay as I get it, have no purse of my own, if I need it I get the keys of the drawers ; I account for all that I may spend of my own free will. I give her my opinion, if needed—I let her see that I appreciate her efforts, and have in her my only companion. I do not take any strong drink on principle; I do not smoke, but that is because I have never learned it, not that I object to it—I consider it a harmless indulgence.

" We find our chief amusement in reading ; I take some little part in the social affairs of the town (I am a native of the town), and the training of our children takes up our time, and we have our friends whom we visit, and who visit us in return and then there is the garden ; we have always plenty to amuse us, the only thing we find is that the time is too short for all that we have to do.

" The children, two of them, are at school, and when they come home and get their home work done for the next day, play about the place ; as our cottage is in the suburbs of the town they have plenty of space and freedom to play with the other children ; the two youngest, one 1 year and 10 months the other 3½ years play about the garden all day long.

" My wife is not a native of the town we are in, she came to it as a domestic servant. Had been a servant from 15 years of age, was 23 years of age when married, and I 24 years, but she had a noble example in her mother who is one of the noblest women I have ever known.

" It may be asked is such a life possible for the majority of men ? I say it advisedly, that it is the fault of 50 per cent. of the skilled artizans (I speak for my own town) that they do not have a home life; there are many men who would think my pay a very small pay indeed, and most of the skilled artizans earn about from 40s. to 60s. per week, and that applies not only to the town I live in, but along the riverside in general.

" It may be asked does the writer of this paper know what poverty is ? There is none knows it better. Up to the age of 15 years I never knew what it was to want anything, but when father died we were left with nothing, and I was just at my trade, and had only 5s. per week. My brother then went to work, and between his pay and mine we managed to scramble through my apprenticeship, but it was a hard struggle for a while. What made it worse was the fact that mother was without the use of one arm and could do very little housework, so that I have had experience of both sides of the question.

" Sir,—When you asked me if I would give you a table such as that I have given, I very readily agreed to do so, for as you well know I was suffering from a very great disappointment, a friend having died at that time whom I would have expected to have saved some money to keep his children from needing help from anyone; indeed it was a great disappointment to many of his friends, but he was not the only one ; there has been five of my fellow workmen died, and they were all in receipt of good wages, from 40s. to 60s. per week—all good workmen and all very intelligent men. Now what was the result after long years of steady work at the pay I have stated above. They left nothing to keep their wife and children—three of them needed to be kept themselves, during their illness, by subscription from their masters and their fellow workmen. Two died somewhat suddenly ; only one had the forethought to insure his life for £100, and that just two years before he died.

" Dear Sir,—This I am sorry to say is an example of 50 per cent. of the present day artizan's life, and I admit it with great regret. The reasons of it are not far to seek. It is so easy to spend an artizan's wage—an hundred times easier, indeed, than it is to save anything from it. Indeed, so much depends upon the wives of working men, that unless they are economical and industrious, and know the science of management, a working man will never get out of the bit. All the money a thriftless wife could get would go, and she would turn round and tell another that she had done well—that she did not know how she could do all she did.

" It is a thing that can be seen every day in life ; two wives of working men, with the same wage to keep house upon, and the same circumstances to deal with. The one can keep her house in comfort and her children a pleasure to look upon, and the other is never comfortable and her house and children are anything but pleasant to see. While thriftlessness plays a large part in keeping many artizans from ever having any means, there is another cause that operates far more, that we see upon our streets and in our police courts—the effects of over-indulgence in strong drink. But that is not where all the evil lies—it is in this so-called moderation (which, I admit, does no harm among those who have the means to afford it), but, Sir, I think I have shown by the tables of expenditure given, that there is no room for such an illegitimate luxury in an artizan's expenditure; even where it is kept within a very small limit, it is still acting indirectly, for it leaves such a small margin of a balance, that it is not thought worth while to save it. Sir, if you—and all like you—who are interested in the welfare of the working class, knew the horrible evil that this thing is working in our midst—morally, physically and financially—you would do all that is in your power to stop the supply; the greatest curse of all is the grocers' license. Sir, it is sapping the womanhood of our country, and if not soon stopped, will work an evil that it will take generations to undo, if ever. If I were asked to give my opinion as to the remedy it would be this: while trying to take away the cause, as I have said above, let the teaching of our womanhood be more direct; teach them the responsibility that attaches to them in their various positions in life, as sisters, as wives and mothers; teach them also the science of management, and this must be done from without, for the present mothers are sadly lacking the qualifications that are needed to teach their daughters; and for the men, well, the same applies to them, if you could only hear as I have heard (when urging them to do something for the sake of their children if not for their wives) the careless remarks that I have been put off with, you would not think I was speaking too strongly in saying they need to be taught their duty as fathers and as husbands. While not seeking to disparage in any way the work of social reform that is going on in our midst—they are all good towards an end, and that is to help them that cannot help themselves; but while that is being done the fact is being overlooked that if those who have the means to help themselves would be taught (or made) to do so, the remainder could be easily looked after. Look at that great meeting held in Glasgow on social reform; in all Lord Rosebery's speech, which, mind you, I agreed with, and thought one of the best I had read on the subject, there was lacking this one element—that personal responsibility of each man making the best of what they have. It is not a pleasant thing to do, but in my opinion it will have to be done in the pulpit, on the platform and in the press, in season and out of season, until it becomes a principle in men to look before them, and not to live only for the day they are in. Presently, if one of themselves exhorts them they will tell him he is a fool, and if a rich man tries they tell him, or rather they say behind his back, that it is all very well for him to speak, although he may have become rich by doing what he wants them to do.

"And as those of us who take an interest in the temperance question have our chief hope in the young, so also will this question need to be dealt with, our young men and our women will need to be taught the principles of thrift, of self-denial and of forethought for themselves and for those who belong to them, and for whom they are responsible.

" This budget is not written for the purpose of showing how little a family can live upon, but rather to show that the average artisan can and ought to be independent of the ordinary troubles and trials of life, unless they should be quite exceptional. That the opposite is the case there is no denying, and I have tried to show the reason for it in the budget. It may be said that what is left over our expenditure is not very large to meet holiday and incidental expense. It is here that the whole thing lies. If there is no preparation made when first entering upon married life, for the extra expense that is sure to come when the children that may be born are growing up to the age at which they are able to help, then the result is a continual grind ; and when the least trouble comes, the parents are unable to meet the additional expense, or, if it is the head of the family, the result is that they are left destitute. If all men that could, would strive to make themselves independent, it would be easy to succour the really poor and unfortunate amongst us."

16.

[SCOTLAND.]   1892.

Painter.   *Children : Boys, ages 12 and 9.*
Wife.   *Girls, ages 11 and 8.*

Number 16 is the budget of a painter in a ship-building yard in ———. He was born in Perthshire, brought up in Stirling, and spent most of his school days in bird's-nesting. His six years' apprenticeship to a painter was disturbed by a plunge into " Geology and Freethinking "—a time when " Shakespeare, Shelley, Byron, and Scott had more charms for him than the Sermon on the Mount." After some years in Edinburgh and London, however, " he returned to his old way of thinking," and became a member of the Free Church of Scotland. He married in Greenock fourteen years ago, with kitchen furniture and 2s. 6d. as his property in hand.

Since his marriage he has been very unfortunate. His wife has had several long illnesses, and his work has been very irregular. When on full time he works fifty-four hours a week, but at the time of his budget he was working only thirty-nine hours. This, at 7¼d. an hour, brings in £1 4s. 4½d. a week, while his eldest boy earns 3s. 6d. a week as message-boy to a jeweller. During the fourteen years of his married life he has been out of work entirely about ten months, and has been on short time—6¾ hours instead of nine hours a day—for about six months. He has saved nothing, but has no debts.

17.

Watchmaker's Assistant.   *Servant : age 14.*
Wife.   *Infant (from 1893).*
Sister-in-law (1893—June, '94).

Number 17 is the budget of a young married couple living in Cambridge. The wife, who was a cook, is well educated, and sews well. The husband is a skilled assistant to a watch-maker at a weekly salary ; he receives in addition a percentage on the sales made. His chief amusements are cycling and music. For these, and also for his own clothes, he pays himself. His wife does not know what his income is, nor whether there are other savings beyond £1 a month for insurance. They have been married three years.

They live in a tastefully furnished little house with a small flower-garden ; two rooms have been occupied for a year by a lodger at 9s. a week. The little maid servant, paid 6s. a month, does not sleep in the house. One friend or another has been with them about ten weeks of the year.

The wife has kept the accounts with no view to publication ; she was accustomed to do so for some years before marriage. They include household expenses and her own personal expenses. Both husband and wife were away from home for three weeks in summer, when no accounts were kept.

By 1893 the family has changed a little ; there is a baby, and a sister of the wife lives with the family ; she works at a shop during the day, but has breakfast and supper at home. At Midsummer they went into a new and larger house, but as it is more in the country they get better accommodation for the same rent as before. The taxes are rather lighter.

The expenses of moving, and of new furniture, were paid by the husband, and are not entered in the accounts.

Note (1894).—The only change in circumstances since last year is that in June the sister who had been lodging, partly boarding with the family, left them. There is a change in the form of saving. The society in which they had been investing during the last few years broke up ; they lost about £46. This year, as is shown, the wife has saved about 10s. a week, and the husband has insured his life. The last item does not appear in the accounts.

RURAL DISTRICTS.

18.

[SOMERSETSHIRE.]　　　　　　　　1892.

Agricultural Labourer, age 45.　　　*Children : Boys, ages* 9, 6 *months.*
Wife,　　　　　*age* 41.　　　　　　*Girls, ages* 13, 7 *and* 5.

Budget 18 is that of an agricultural labourer in Somersetshire. He was born in Devon, came to Somersetshire about nineteen years ago in search of work, and has been ever since with his present employer. He has been married eighteen years. Besides the five children at home, there are three others away—two girls of sixteen and eighteen, at service in the neighbourhood, and a son of twenty-one, a cripple from birth, who has been apprenticed to a boot-maker by the Board of Guardians. The wife earns nothing beyond the proceeds of a few pairs of stockings she knits in the year and sells to the neighbours.

The husband's work is not that of the ordinary farm labourer ; his employer lives five miles away on another farm, leaving the man in charge of a farm of 220 acres and a flock of sheep sometimes numbering from three to four hundred. No other labour is regularly employed on the farm, of which, for the last six years, only fourteen acres have been arable. His hours are from seven a.m. to five p.m., but he is often at work longer ; half-an-hour is allowed for breakfast at eight o'clock, and an hour for dinner at one o'clock. He does hedging in overtime, getting in return the wood he cuts for firewood. His wages, 11s. a week, are paid fortnightly. He has no money perquisites, but in addition to his right to firewood, he has a rent-free house and a garden of three-eighths of an acre. He realizes a net profit of about 10s. a year on the sale of his pig in February; he buys the pig from his employer in October for about 17s., the price being deducted from his wages at the rate of 1s. or more per week. He keeps fowls, and generally sells his chickens and also eggs, unless the price is as low as 7d. a dozen or under. His gross annual income is not more than £37.

He lives in an old farmhouse, too large for his needs—three of the six bedrooms are not used ; there are also two kitchens and a parlour. The food consists chiefly of tea, bread, butter, and potatoes ; bacon at nearly every meal, vegetables and pudding at dinner. Fresh meat is never eaten.

19.

[SOMERSETSHIRE.]　　　　　　　　1892.

Agricultural Labourer, age 46.　　　*Children : Boys, ages* 19, 12 *and* 6.
Wife,　　　　　*age* 41.　　　　　　*Girls, ages* 10, 8 *and* 1.

The second agricultural labourer was born and brought up in a Somersetshire village, six miles from his present home. The only time he has been out of the district was when, at twenty-three years of age, he made a two years' tour through England, visiting Wales, Yorkshire, Bristol, and London, partly to look for work, partly to see the country. He worked in iron mines till he was thirty-nine years of age. Seven years ago, on the close of the mines, he got work on a farm, at first in his native place. He has been four years with his present employer.

The farm is 300 acres in extent, 200 acres arable, 26 meadow, and the rest pasture. Two other men are employed, one of them a horse-driver; also two boys, one to drive the horses, the other as cow-boy. The farmer would employ more regular hands if he could get them. At haymaking and harvest he has extra men. The hours are, as usual, from seven o'clock till five, and longer at haymaking and harvest. The man breakfasts before starting, at six o'clock, and takes lunch and dinner of bread and cheese or bacon from home; he has tea at home and a hot supper at eight o'clock. They use fresh meat "once a year," but have bacon two or three times a day.

They live two miles from the husband's work, in an old farm-house very much out of repair and scantily furnished; there are two kitchens, four small bedrooms, and a dairy. The net value of the produce of the garden amounts to about 30s. a year. The man keeps pigs and fowls, and gets £1 extra at harvest and 4s. at haymaking.

He has been married twenty-two years. One son, twenty-one years of age, is a private in a line regiment stationed in Upper Burmah; a girl of seventeen is a housemaid in a private school in the neighbouring town, and another, a girl of fifteen, is in farm service near. One boy of nineteen living at home does odd work on the farm; he gets 12s. a week wages, of which he gives 5s. for bed and board.

The man is a teetotaller, but until recently was allowed nothing at harvest and other times instead of beer; now he has 1s. a week extra from Lady-Day to Michaelmas. He is a keen politician—a Radical, and a member of the Village Liberal Committee.

20.

Woodman and Gardener, age 45.	*Children* : *Boys, ages* 9 *and* 7.
Wife *age* 49.	*Girls, ages* 5 *and* 3.

Budget 20 is that of a woodman and gardener in Somerset-shire. He was born in the district, and has lived there all his life. He has worked on the land since a child of seven, when he earned 3d. a day. When ten years of age he went to live in farm service. He has been woodman and gardener to his present employer for twenty-one years. His wife was also born and brought up in the district. Both husband and wife have been married before, the wife to an ironstone worker in the neighbouring mines; her three sons by her first marriage are miners, her one daughter is in service. The husband's children by his first wife are also away

D

from home, two girls in service, one boy a private in a line regiment, and another learning electrical engineering.

The wife earns 5s. a week by working as laundress to her husband's master. The husband's hours are from 8 a.m. to 6 p.m., with half-an-hour for lunch and one hour for dinner. For lunch and dinner he carries with him from home, bread and cheese, cold salt meat and tea. In addition to the usual bread and butter and tea for breakfast, they have bacon, potatoes, and sometimes eggs ; and for their hot supper at seven o'clock they occasionally have even a little fresh meat.

The man makes a profit of £1 6s. a year on his pig, and also earns a few pounds in the year by repairing clocks and watches in the evenings. He is a very well-read and intelligent man ; a Radical and a member of the Village Liberal Committee.

They live in a good, comfortably furnished cottage, and, although another family lives under the same roof, have for their own use a kitchen, pantry, and three bedrooms. The garden produces enough potatoes and vegetables to last all the year.

21.

[SURREY.]

Labourer and Gardener.   *Children, Son (1).*
Wife.   *Girls (5).*

Budget 21 is that of a gardener in Surrey, living in the same district as the widow in monograph 22. He was born in a neighbouring parish. There he was a labourer and gardener until, about fifteen years ago, he migrated with his present employer to the village where he now lives. Besides the six children at home, there are four daughters in service ; the eldest son is a gardener in a distant part of the country, and the second son in a neighbouring village. The third son is at home, apprenticed to his uncle, a carpenter. The fifth daughter helps at home, and earns enough in summer to buy her own clothes. The four younger ones are at school.

In addition to his wages, 25s. a week, the man has his house rent free, and coals and lighting ; a gun license, given by his employer, enables him to provide the household with rabbits. The wife earns some pounds in summer by washing. The children away from home do not, perhaps, make any regular contribution, but probably give presents.

22.

[SURREY.]

Widow, age 80.   *[Grandchild, age 10.]*

Budget 22 is that of an old widow living in a solitary cottage on the southern borders of Surrey. She was born and brought up in the district, and has never been further away than Chichester.

Her husband was of yeoman stock. He worked as "useful" man at the place where his wife was dairy-maid, and by middle life became working bailiff on a small estate. Of their five children two are living. The eldest son is a struggling farmer in the valley, with a wife and several young children. A daughter, now a widow, lives in the neighbouring village. On her husband's death, two year's ago, the old widow was persuaded to live with her son, but the air of the valley "choked her," and she "pined and dwined away" for want of her hillside home. She returned to the old cottage where she had lived for nearly sixty years, and has been there ever since. She does her own household work, and a little grandchild who comes after school hours to spend the night with her, is her main source of communication with the outer world.

Her own and her husband's savings were spent in setting up their son in his farm, and now she lives rent free, with occasional help from him, on a pension of 3s. 6d. a week from her former employers.

23.

[SUSSEX.] 1892.

Journeyman Carpenter.   *Children : Girls, ages 15, 13 and 11.*
Wife.

Budget 23 is that of a Sussex journeyman carpenter. He has been married nineteen years; has followed his present occupation for twenty-five years, and has been with his present employer fourteen years. He supplies his own files and tools at a cost of £1 a year. The family makes about £5 a year by hop-picking, in addition to the father's weekly wages. They live in a very small four-room cottage, and have a garden, the produce of which is worth about £1 a year.

24.

[CUMBERLAND.] 1892.

Bobbin Turner, age 30.   *Children : Boy, age 3 (until death).*
Wife   age 28.   *Girl, age 5.*

Budget 24 is that of a married couple living near Keswick. The man's parents were Cumbrians, and, as a boy, he went to work at a bobbin mill. He ran away when nineteen in order to enlist, but was not accepted as he had lost the sight of an eye. He returned to his old work and when twenty-three, having saved £25, he married. He has been married six years, and of the two children one is alive, the other having died in May of the year covered by the accounts.

The husband's wages have been about 21s. a week, but in addition to that, his wife has been able to go out charing and washing a great deal, which has helped to make the income considerably greater. The man neither smokes nor drinks, and usually gives his wife his entire wages.

The house stands on the main street of the village. There are practically only two rooms, but upstairs the small landing holds a bed comfortably. From September this was let to a brother, who, with the exception of a month at Christmas, when he paid at the rate of 15s., paid 10s. a week for board and lodging.

The health of the man has on the whole been good, but when absent from work through illness he receives 9s. a week from a Mechanics' club.

The husband takes his breakfast and dinner with him, but has his tea at home at six p.m., which often consists of meat and vegetables. They pay about 7s. a week in subscriptions to various clubs—Mechanics', British Workman's, Coaling and Clothing, and two Building Clubs. Generally both husband and wife go away for a holiday when the mill is closed during Whitsun week.

NOTES ON SOME OF THE CHARACTERISTICS OF THE VILLAGE OF WHITESTONE.

(By the Compiler of Budgets Nos. 25, 26, 27 and 28. 1891.)

With a view to make the information given in the four following monographs more complete, I have put down a few details describing the village to which all the four families (Nos. 25, 26, 27 and 28) whose budgets are given belong.

Whitestone is a fair-sized village, lying prettily enough among fields and hedgerows, but depending for its support very little upon agricultural labour. The occupation given to its people comes almost entirely from the coal pits, which extend far and wide beneath its cottages and lanes. In olden times, before the mines were worked, it was a weaving village, and though but few traces of this old industry remain, there may still be found in one or two of the larger cottages an old hand-loom more or less out of repair. The only surviving relic of the old occupation is the "seaming" stockings and socks, done by the women. These articles leave the loom in one flat piece, and are sewn into the requisite shape by hand. In the old days, they were made in hand-looms in the village itself, but there are few such looms remaining in the cottages now. The stocking making is done in large factories in the neighbourhood. The stockings in their flat condition are despatched from the factories to women in the surrounding villages, who undertake to have them "seamed," and give out this work to the cottage housewives. After seaming, the stockings are collected again, and sent in to the dyers. The work is very ill-paid, being largely done by married women in their leisure hours. The skill required for it is soon gained ; and no implement is needed but a needle. The wool with which the seam is worked is always supplied from the factory, as it is most important that it should be of precisely the same quality and kind as that used for the weaving of the stockings. Otherwise there is a danger lest, after the process of dyeing, a difference between the fabric and the stitches of the seam might make itself visible. Several years ago, one woman in the village seamed her stockings with thread or wool of her own supplying. Nothing was known until several weeks later, when the women went as usual to take their week's supply of work from the undertaker or "sweater." She told them that she had none to give. The factory managers had written to say that complaints of the seaming had been received from the dye works. The work complained of had been part of that sent from Whitestone, and the factory had determined to give out no more work to be seamed there. The consternation was great, especially among the widows and spinsters dependent on earnings of their own. Representations were made, and after a few weeks the factory manager relented. The prices paid vary from 8d. a dozen pairs for long stockings down to 4d. and 3d. for socks; even to 2½d. for the very coarse and common kinds. Little children do a great deal of this seaming, and it is characteristic of Whitestone to see the women standing at their doors with a pile of stockings thrown over the left shoulder, while they chat and look about them, their hands busily employed picking up the seam stitches, working with a peculiar motion difficult to unlearn when they have other kinds of sewing to do, and the habit of which brings the children into periodic trouble with the school inspector, the code requiring not only neat execution but a proper way of holding the needle in the hand.

Even this home industry bids fair to become obsolete, as some new inventions in machinery enable the weavers to manufacture the hose and vests in circular shape without any seam at all, so that the factory managers need have no recourse to hand needlework.

A large number of the girls and young women work at an Elastic Factory, some of the men at an iron foundry, and some at brickmaking; but the main source of livelihood for the village comes from the pits.

There are the highly trained colliers, " the proper colliers with the pick," the colliers' labourers, who work with and under these in the actual labour of detaching the coal, there are the men who mind the horses, the men who see to the trucks, the labourers on the pit bank, the colliery bricklayers and stable attendants above ground, the hauliers, clerks and superintendents.

The colliers, properly so called, receive a monthly allowance of 16 cwt. of coal. They pay for the hauling, which costs 2s. a load (16 cwt.) from the pit's mouth to Whitestone. The banksmen have simply the privilege of buying their coal cheap. They pay for coal delivered at their cottage doors 6s. a load, or 7s. a ton. The villagers, who have to buy coal without this privilege, pay 9d. and 9½d. a cwt.

The home of these people is not an unattractive one. The air is light and invigorating, the air of the Midlands redeemed from flatness by the neighbourhood of moorland and forest. The ground about the place, though not strikingly beautiful, is well broken. There is the interest of hill and valley, brook and wood, with peeps of widely stretching landscape bounded by distant hills. The village proper consists mainly of one long irregular winding street, beginning in low lying ground, and meandering past schools, church, and one or two chapels, up to a dreary space of ground dignified as " the green," but with hardly a patch of grass remaining on it, then running up hill, and abutting on to a cross road, the boundary between Whitestone and a neighbouring village.

Along one side of the cross road and down the hill again are more Whitestone cottages, clustering round a brook and a well. The well has no pump, and the buckets dipped into it at random are often foul, spreading impurity and causing illness. If fever is about, and gets a chance, it rages here. Otherwise illness is not common, for the place is healthy, and if the cottages present a somewhat dull and formal red brick face to the village street, a step to the back will show them to be picturesque and pleasant. There are good gardens well supplied with vegetables. Sufficient room for clothes lines and drying, and in most cases a bed or two of garden flowers. The colliers are very fond of flowers, and many cultivate them carefully and with good success.

The gardens and the country beyond make a wholesome background, and though there is at Whitestone a sad want of enlightened views as to the opening of windows, especially bedroom windows, the doors stand mostly open at back and front, and the air finds its way into the recesses of the small homes pretty thoroughly.

Inside the houses are not too charming. Perhaps it is on account of the seaming, which continually occupies the women, who are rarely seen at their doors without a stocking foot drawn over the left hand, a needle in the right, and a skein of wool thrown over the shoulder; perhaps it is on account of this constant preoccupation over the duty of making up the rent of the house rather than on that of adorning it; but certain it is that neither the dainty charm of a south country cottage nor the well ordered and solid comfort of a northern homestead are often to be seen.

There is a lack of the brilliant polish of the wood, the spotless cleanliness of the floor which are the pride of the northern housewife, but in the better sort of homes there are still some indications of the varied tastes and artistic needs. Handsome bibles and bound volumes of religious periodicals, china and glass ornaments, or the bead-work trophies of school girl dexterity abound, and where-ever the family live there is at least always the charm of a good fire.

The people themselves have generally warm kind hearts. They are easy to talk with, easy to please ; I am speaking principally of the women, as I know them much better than the men, at least in their every day life and aspect. The men I see when accident or old age or illness keeps them at home, not often other-wise. I should say that they were less ready to accept a stranger and to credit him with good intentions than their wives, less easy and natural in manner, and more conscious of differences of rank, but when the outer crust thaws, they shew well. They seem fond of their children, and, with one or two black exceptions, are fairly kind to their wives, who have, however, a hard time of it, with little relief or pleasure beyond the one inalienable, invaluable privilege of gossip.

When good health prevails, and the heads of the family do not drink, a very fair standard of solid comfort prevails. There would seem to be no lack of food, and, on gala occasions, the children and young folk turn out exceedingly well dressed.

The men are mostly vigorous and well grown, this is in part owing to the fact that of late years the colliers have been rarely overworked. Work has, indeed, been often sadly short, especially in the summer of 1887. For the coal at White-stone being of the best kind suitable for private house consumption, a long hot summer, such as the Jubilee summer was, seriously affects the demand. The mines are dry, and much less dangerous than most. There is no fire-damp. But the calling necessarily involves continual small hazards. The colliery owners seem to be fairly liberal in their treatment of accidents within the limits of their own responsibility ; but many fall outside this line. The men grow reckless about dangers which are daily faced, and when they are hurt by their own fault they and their families have often much hardship to go through, only very partially relieved by the action of the Friendly Societies. There is rarely anything laid by in addition, the usual plan being to obtain credit with the shops in summer, and become a little, often not a little, in debt before the winter, when four and even five days' work a week may be counted on to help to straighten accounts. The memories of the colliers, however, are reported to be very faulty with regard to past indebtedness, and they seem to have a truly aristocratic horror of a dun.

The hours of work are short, $7\frac{1}{2}$ to $8\frac{1}{2}$ hours actually below ground, but the long walks in all weathers to and from work make a serious addition, especially for those not constitutionally robust.

The colliers spend their leisure time in working at their plots of garden or their allotments, in summer a good deal also in cricket, and a good deal always in sauntering and chatting. Of late, after two successful contests with the masters, they have been very well off, and have had plenty to spend on such amusements as they care for. Among the worse sort, betting and immoderate drinking have prevented their prosperity from being of lasting good, but the better men have added perceptibly to the family comfort. Perambulators have become a common sight.

There are in the village ten houses licensed for the sale of drink, one general drapery shop, and six for the sale of chandlery, groceries and bread. The farmers sell meat and milk to such as want it. There is a post office for letters, not for telegrams or money orders. There is no resident doctor in the village, no family above the lower middle class, and no minister of religion except the Church of England clergyman. It is difficult to form an estimate of the number of people who pay serious allegiance to the established religion of the country. The attendance in church on Sunday morning is almost *nil*. In the evening it is a trifle, but not much better. On the way to church, on Sunday morning, one may meet group after group of men walking away towards the open country. Sometimes they have their younger children with them, and are, no doubt, fulfilling the duty of keeping them out of the way of the " Missus," whilst she is absorbed in the grand task of preparing dinner. The people, as a rule, welcome the clergyman to their houses, extol his kindness, sympathise with his family anxieties and pleasures, and in all distress invoke his aid with confidence. But their adherence to his religion is not of that vigorous kind which prompts self-sacrifice. On the other hand, the Wesleyans, Primitive Methodists and Particular Baptists make considerable efforts to render their services decent and popular. The principal members of each flock provide the minister's Sunday dinner and tea, and see to his comfort when, on special occasions, he visits Whitestone for a service in the course of the week.

The ministers on their side are most energetic on occasions of school treats or prize givings. They distribute tea and buns, direct the games, and preside over class leaders and choir, when, at the end of a day's pleasure, the whole party of holiday makers will gather together, after our serious English fashion, "to conclude with the Doxology."

There are few Roman Catholics in Whitestone proper, and no chapel nearer than that at the neighbouring village where there is a large colony of Irish people.

Politics are not vehemently disputed. There is a lack of intellectual life, and a great lack of the means of supplying intellectual needs. Few of the colliers take a daily paper or appear to be much interested in the concerns of the world outside Whitestone.

Second Note on the Village of Whitestone (1892).

The condition of the village, generally, is much the same as in 1891. The colliers are prosperous, and there is little or no want of employment. It may be noted that in 1890 there was only one case of indoor relief, that of a girl of seventeen, who had given her parents (respectable people) much trouble. She would not stay in service, but ran away and slept in barns. After entering the workhouse she behaved well. Out relief was given to twelve aged people, to one widow of 42 with a large family, to one woman suffering from "dementia," but cared for by her family, and to one man with an ulcerated foot. Medical relief is easy to obtain in Whitestone, and old people of good character are generally allowed out relief when they apply for it.

There is a branch of a co-operative society at a village two miles from Whitestone, but it does not yet obtain much custom at Whitestone itself; having to fight against the influences of the complicated evils of the long credit system adopted in the village shops.

Note on Whitestone—January, 1896.

Since this village was described in 1892 it has gone through some changes. The colliery strike of the summer and autumn of 1893 has been its most remarkable event. The strike of the miners threw out of employment all those not miners who are employed about a colliery—stablemen, banksmen, blacksmiths, hauliers, &c. These lost work from the beginning of the strike, and within a few weeks from this date the want of coal caused a stoppage also in the work at the elastic and mosaic factories, and at the iron foundry; the labourers and operatives in these employments, of course, receiving no strike pay. The miners received 7/- a week each, with an extra allowance of 1/- a week for each child under working age. This money was paid at a village two miles off on market night to the men, a plan causing much temptation to expenditure and drink; so that in many cases little of the money reached the households at Whitestone. This pay altogether ceased after the strike had been going on for some weeks, and, practically, the whole population of the village became dependent upon the kindness of the shops or of benevolent friends. The Roman Catholic Priest and a Dissenting Minister of the neighbouring village organised relief; neighbours and friends gave in various ways, and loaves were distributed pretty freely, but in the last weeks many were insufficiently fed, and as the autumn drew on the want of coal became a serious hardship. The strike ended in a victory for the men. After this, there was a short period of very good work, but before Christmas a period of depression came on, which has lasted almost uninterruptedly through 1894 and 1895.

The credit system, the complicated evils of which were referred to in the note for 1892, was of infinite value to the miners during the strike. The shops which had the advantage of their regular custom were expected to continue to provide the necessaries of life, and actually did provide them to a surprising extent, although the tradespeople felt great doubts as to the likelihood of ultimate repayment. Partly, they were, no doubt, influenced by good nature and neighbourly feeling. They reckoned up the cost, however, and knowing that they stood to lose in any case by the strike, preferred to hazard present cash rather than the popularity on which future receipts would have to depend. The Co-operative Society of the neighbouring village, however, stuck to its principles, gave no credit, but allowed its members to draw to the extent of the value of their share capital, and, though with some difficulty, weathered the storm.

Of the families described in the four Whitestone monographs, the Hunters (No. 28) are fairly flourishing. In fact the Primitive Methodists, as a body, are doing well. They have some fresh members among families lately settled in some new houses in the village. They are mostly thrifty and temperate people, and the body is planning the erection of a new and superior chapel.

The Forts (No. 27) are less prosperous. Fort has only brought his wife four shillings in the course of the last year. He has bad health, occasional times of real illness from bronchitis and cold, and his irregular habits increase. His wife and youngest daughter work hard to maintain themselves and him, and the youngest boy is now earning moderate wages and is good to his mother.

The collier's family (No. 26) described has suffered from the depression in his trade. His wife complains much of the altered times.

25.

[BY THE COMPILER. FICTITIOUS NAMES HAVE BEEN USED.]

Boot Maker.   *Boy, age 12.*
Wife.

The family consists of Welldon and his wife, hardly arrived at middle age, and a son of twelve years old, who has just passed his sixth standard at the National School. An older girl (about 20) is the only other child. She used to be a pupil teacher at the same school, and to live at home, but is now an assistant mistress at a school at a distance. Welldon was an orphan brought up in the union, and apprenticed by the parish authorities to the boot-making trade, which he has pursued ever since. He is a steady, respectable man, cheerful tempered and active, but not very strong in health. He is a particularly kind husband and father, took great pride in the school achievements of his daughter, and was an excellent nurse to his wife during a long illness, and to one of his children who was severely scalded and ill a long time. Two children are dead.

For many years Welldon worked at boot-making in his own house and on his own account, but was forced to give up this about four years ago owing to bad debts. The people would not pay, and Mrs. Welldon says that she and her husband were nearly " stripped bare of all," before they decided to give up. Welldon took work under a master boot-maker in the neighbourhood. It was at this time that I first became acquainted with the family, when the wife was very ill, her illness being brought on partly by grief for the loss of a little child, partly by worry about money matters. I never suspected the latter cause, as the house —a good four-roomed cottage—is always beautifully kept; the furniture good and spotlessly clean, ornaments and pictures in abundance on the walls and shelves, and the woman's bed-room during her illness perfectly neat and clean.

When Welldon left off business on his own account, he had to pay off a good deal of debt. This burden was a trying one, but is lifted now, and the family is clear of the world. Welldon makes from 15s. a week to something over a pound at his work. A little extra money comes in once a fortnight when he goes round on behalf of the doctor to collect subscriptions to his medical club; to which a regular payment secures attendance and medicine in time of sickness. He is a Forester, and very active in the management of the local lodge, expressing an opinion that the Foresters could set an example to the Houses of Parliament by the way in which they transact business, without unnecessary fuss or more talk than is absolutely needed. He is above the level of the people round him in intelligence.

His wife is refined and gentle, but not clever, but his daughter is remarkably so. The latter was very successful as a pupil teacher, and is reported to be doing excellent work at the school where she now teaches. If the children do not come clean to school, she takes them down to the cellar (where appliances for washing are kept) and scrubs them well. At Whitestone school, she used to beg her mother for old garments and boots to be made as good as could be for the poor and neglected children of the school. The Welldons are very charitable. A poor old crippled neighbour of theirs, who lives on 2s. 6d. a week from the parish, and what she can earn by mending the colliers' breeches and shirts when their wives are busy, tells me that Mrs. Welldon looks in every day to see what she can do for her, and that the little boy fetches her a bucket of water from the well before he goes to school in the morning. The Welldons keep a pig, and have never been without one, though at times it has been hard to find food enough for it. They have a small piece of ground besides their own garden, and grow potatoes and vegetables and some fruit.

Mrs. Welldon is rather a low-spirited woman, of very delicate health. She and her husband have made a gallant fight against misfortune, never looking poor or asking help, with the result that she is a little embittered. She lives surrounded by many neighbours who waste their money in drink, look miserable, and ask for assistance at the first breath of trouble. She says that many of the parents who send their children ill-clothed and not fed to school, could afford to make them thoroughly comfortable, if it were not for the drink.

The method of life of the Welldons is a little unlike that of their neighbours, who are either colliers or employed on work connected with the pit. Welldon does not leave home as they do in the middle of the night, and the family sits down to an orderly and substantial breakfast, at which their own home-cured bacon generally figures. They are proud of its excellence, and when their daughter Lizzie left home to live at a distance, she specially begged that her parents would find her in bacon. The mother demurred, she told me, but the father, without saying anything, went out, and cut her a good sized piece from the side hanging up. At the time of the accounts, however, the family seem to have been buying bacon.

The rent covers the sum paid for the extra piece of land taken by Welldon, in addition to his cottage garden. No article seems to have been purchased oftener than once a week, except sugar, when in the third week an extra quantity was procured when Mrs. Welldon was making jam from some of her garden fruit. On one occasion the detailed accounts showed a sum of 13s. 8d. paid all at once for coal; this was characteristic of the family, the large expense having been no doubt anticipated and prepared for.

Little change has taken place in the circumstances of this family since 1891. The man still works at shoe-making, earning 4s. a day when in work, but cannot count on making six days in the week. The family has moved from the cottage formerly inhabited into a fresh one, new and well-built, with good ventilation. It has a pleasant sitting-room, a kitchen, and two upstairs bed-rooms. At the back, across an open space, is an outhouse with conveniencies for washing. Mrs. Welldon washes at home. There is also a pig-sty, and a good sized piece of ground planted with vegetables, with borders of flowers.

The family breakfasts at 7 a.m., on bread and butter and bacon and tea. The man takes with him to his work his dinner, consisting of cold meat and bread, and a slice of cake. At 12.30 p.m., after the return of the son from school, he and his mother dine together, and have tea at 4.30 p.m. At 6.30 p.m. Welldon has tea, sometimes with meat and potatoes, but oftener not.

Before going to bed the son has some bread and cheese, or a little fruit pie or cake, but his father rarely takes anything after the 6.30 tea. Mrs. Welldon takes some bread and cheese with her son if she feels inclined.

During the time covered by the accounts, the price of eggs rose, being first sixteen, then fourteen, and finally ten a shilling.

The Foresters' Club gives benefit for the man to the amount of 10s. a week in sickness, for 26 weeks; 5s. a week for a second 26 weeks; and in case of continuous disabling illness 2s. 6d. a week through life.

The landlord of the Welldons used to be a neighbouring publican. They moved because he wanted to raise the rent 1s. a week. They now live under a cousin of Mrs. Welldon's, who has a shop for fancy goods at the sea-side, and owns land at Whitestone on which he has built thirteen cottages, including the one occupied by the Welldons.

26.

[LEICESTERSHIRE.]   1891.

Collier.   Children : Sons, ages 19 and 13.
Wife.   Girl, age 4.

Budget 26, for two periods, the autumns of 1891 and 1892, is that of a collier in a Leicestershire village. His son, a colliery labourer, died in the interval between the two periods. The father has been at pit work for about thirty-seven years—since he was seven years old. He and his son were supposed in the village to earn £3 a week between them, of which the father contributed 15s. to 17s. a week, and the son 10s., to the household. Both clothed themselves from their reserve funds.

There is a daughter, married, in the village, and two younger children at home. The wife distributes out-door relief as agent to the relieving officer.

The house looks on the village green—a desolate patch. It has one large room, living room and kitchen combined, on the ground floor, and a scullery. Above the living room is a bedroom, and another above that. The garden in front, across the road, supplies potatoes and vegetables for about half the year.

The customs of the family, with regard to meals, are the same as those of the other collier households in the village (*cf.* No. 27b).

The groceries and chandlery were not classified for the first three weeks of the period covered by the budget; the sum has been distributed in the tables between the various items on the same scale as in the remaining weeks.

27.

[LEICESTERSHIRE.]   1891.

[BY THE COMPILER   FICTITIOUS NAMES HAVE BEEN USED.]

Colliery Groom.	*Sons, ages* 22 *and* 17.
Wife.	*Daughters, ages* 19 *and* 13.

The family consists of six members.   Fort, the father, works as a groom at the neighouring colliery.   In former days he was a gentleman's coachman, and subsequently for some time coachman at an inn.   His wife says that he has seen foreign parts and America, but in what capacity he travelled, I failed to discover. He bears the character amòng his neighbours of being a good, easy man, kind enough to his wife, but "one who would never notice if she clemmed,* as long as he had a good dinner himself," as a neighbour remarked to me.   I suspeƈt that irregular habits. or too much easy going have contributed to prevent him from doing as well in the world as he might have done.   His position seems low for a man of his age, especially one of whose cleverness and experience his wife speaks so highly, and who has had opportunities as a servant.   Perhaps all he does, or rather all he makes, does not make itself entirely known to his family.   Mrs. Fort does a little "seaming," (*cf.* note, p. 52) but is mainly occupied with the care of her family.   She is a helpful neighbour also, and I have often found her churning, or making up butter, or cutting out a garment for a village friend.   She is also a ready helper in the household of her eldest son, who is married, and lives close to her.   She papered and whitewashed his cottage, and I found her this summer energetically performing the same good office for her own.   George, the elder son, works as a blacksmith's stoker at the pit, he pays for his own clothes, and pays his mother 15s. a week.   Charles, the younger boy, is apprenticed to a boot maker.   He pays his mother 6s. weekly.   Next year he hopes to make his contribution 7s. With what he keeps for himself, he pays for his own clothes, except boots, which his master provides, gratis.   The master also helps with other clothes, but I think that this is beyond his contraƈt, and is only a matter of kindness and good feeling.   Ellen, the elder daughter, is a dressmaker, just setting up.   She provides for her own clothes, and pays her mother what she can for board.   She is helped in her work by Patty, the youngest child, who is still at school ; but is able to devote the early mornings and a little time in the evening to sewing the easier parts of Ellen's work.   Later on she will, probably, pursue the same calling, as she is fond of her needle, and is already distinguishing herself at school in this subjeƈt ; gaining a prize of 1s. 6d. for a piece of neat plain work. Ellen was a pupil teacher at Whitestone school for some time after ceasing to be a scholar, but did not care for the occupation, and wished to be apprenticed to the dressmaking.   Her apprenticeship fee was paid for in part by a grant of £9 from a local charity, the proceeds of which are divided between four neighbouring villages.

Each village takes its turn in the enjoyment of a year's income of this charity, which provides for the apprenticeship of poor and

---

* Clemmed=Starved.

deserving girls. A similar charity helped Charles with his apprenticeship to the boot-maker.

George is a well grown, active-looking young man. Ellen
used to look anæmic and under-fed, but has lately become far
more rosy and healthy in appearance. During the years of her
apprenticeship, her hours were very long, and she suffered from
the heat of the workroom and the want of fresh air. Now she
says that she is her own mistress, and though she has to work early
and late, she can vary the monotony of needlework by a chat at
the door with a friend, an errand for a neighbour, or a turn at
helping her mother in the house. She was engaged during the
time covered by the accounts, in making several dresses for neighbours, and was proud of having to make those of the young
daughters' of a neighbouring publican, and of having the good
word of the village blacksmith and his wife, at whose house she
had spent a week, sewing and making up clothes for the family.
She takes in two fashion books, each costing 1d. a month. These,
besides being of use to her in her trade, are much enjoyed as
general literature by her mother and sister, as well as herself, and
are produced for the entertainment of visitors.

The manners of the family are very gentle and affectionate ;
much more so than is common at Whitestone. They occupy an
excellent four-roomed cottage, for which they pay 2s. a week.
The rates are paid by their landlord. They occupied until lately,
a low gloomy cottage, for which they paid the same rent, and rates
in addition. This cottage had no windows at the back. It faced
north, and its windows and door opened opposite to a farm yard,
where manure heaps were constantly stacked within a few yards
of the cottage. The Forts used to suffer from a chronic low state
of health, and are now very full of the enjoyment they derive from
freer air and more sunshine, as well as from a greater feeling of
health and appetite.

The total income at the disposal of Mrs. Fort consists of the
contributions from George and Charles, already mentioned, 15s. a
week and 6s. a week, respectively ; an uncertain but probably
small contribution from Ellen, and a sum from Fort himself, which
varies from 9s. to 12s., and occasionally reaches as much as 15s.
when special expenses have to be met. He makes 3s. a day at the
colliery stable, but there is not always a full week's work for him.*
He makes a little extra money by horse clipping, for which purpose he owns two clipping machines, one of which cost 8s. 6d. and
the other 12s. 6d.

The prices paid by Mrs. Fort for goods are the same as those
given at the end of the monograph No. 27, as current in Whitestone village. The meat is all fresh meat at 8d. a pound, with the
exception of one purchase of a tin of corned beef for 11d. The
amount spent for liquid nourishment seems extraordinary small, if
not quite inadequate. Possibly the tea and coffee is consumed
mainly by the three female members of the family. The Forts are
not peculiar in abstaining from milk. At Whitestone it is very
unusual among the people to drink it with tea, and I know of one
well-to-do family in which there are four young children, and

---

* The colliery owners keep back something out of his wages, as a contribution to a fund which
gives 7s. a week to all men, employed by them, who are hurt at their work.

where no milk is ever taken. The small farmers have no market for their skim milk, and it is largely given to the pigs. The absence of a charge for vegetables is accounted for, as in the case of the Hunter family, by the fact that the Forts have a garden yielding potatoes and vegetables in sufficient quantity. In their case it is more difficult than in that of Hunter, to make out a satisfactory balance sheet; Fort's contribution to the family income being irregular, and Ellen's unknown to me. Omitting the latter, which is very small and uncertain, and taking Fort's at the lowest sum mentioned by his wife, the expenditure for the six weeks would exceed the income by a sum of 18s. 1d.

List of the articles purchased oftener than once a week :—

Bread was bought 26 times in 6 weeks.

Flour	,,	24	,,	,,
Butter	,,	24	,,	,,
Sugar	,,	14	,,	,,
Cheese	,,	15	,,	,,
Meat	,,	7	,,	,,
Bacon	,,	12	,,	,,
Tea	,,	7	,,	,,
Oil	,,	12	,,	,,

Note by Compiler, 1892 (27 *b*).[*]

Since 1891, George Fort and Ellen have both married, and are no longer members of their father's household. George's contribution of 15s. a week is greatly missed by the mother, who spoke gratefully, however, of his kindness in having paid for a load of coal in the summer, and having given her 2s. 6d. one day. In the good days, before George married, and still more before the marriage of the eldest son, Tom, Mrs. Fort s housekeeping was conducted on a more liberal scale than now. The whole family sat down regularly to a good meat meal at 5 p.m. on the return of the men from work. Now a poorer *régime* prevails. Fort's work has been slack; during the week preceeding the six weeks of which the expenses are given above, he only made 5s. The woman does all she can; has been hay-making, charing, washing, nursing, and sewing for neighbours. The people at the neighbouring public house are kina, and give her a day's work whenever they can, when she gets her food and a little money.

At present the habits of the Forts, as to meals, are not unlike those of the Hunters. Fort gets his breakfast for himself early, and takes bread with butter or bacon for his 11 a.m. "snap." Mrs. Fort and Patty breakfast at 8.30, and take dinner, consisting of bread with dripping or cheese or bacon, at one. At five the man returns, and a dinner of meat and potatoes and pudding is cooked for him ; his wife and Patty partake, if there is enough ; if not they eat potatoes and "what there is." A supper of bread and cheese is eaten at 8.30 p.m.

Patty earns nothing, but helps her mother, either by undertaking the household work when her mother is out at any of the employments mentioned above, or by doing the easier parts of dressmaking for neighbours, undertaken occasionally by her mother.

The landlord of the Forts is a farmer, born in the village. His father was a good workman, who saved money. His wife seems to take the most active part in looking after his tenants, collects the rent, and inspects the premises, to see that they are properly kept. Mrs. Fort asked her if she would allow her something in consideration of her having papered and whitewashed the cottage herself, "It is an improvement" she urged. "Yes, but you get the benefit of it yourself, my wench," replied the landlady. She is, however, on good terms with her tenants, and assures them that they may count on not being turned out if they pay their rent regularly.

The club to which Mrs. Fort contibutes 1s. a fortnight is on her youngest son's behalf, (learning to be a bootmaker, as described in 1891). The benefits are 10s. a week in sickness, for twenty weeks, then 5s., and £10 at death.

---

[*] For further particulars (1896) see page 56.

18.

[BY THE COMPILER. FICTITIOUS NAMES HAVE BEEN USED.]

Colliery Blacksmith.   *Children : Son, age 22.*
Wife.   *Daughters, ages 25 and 14.*

The family whose expenditure for six weeks is given in the
accompanying sheet, resides in Leicestershire, in a village which
may be called Whitestone, and consists of five members: Hunter
and his wife, both elderly people, a daughter, Mary, aged twenty-
five, a son William, aged twenty-two, and a younger daughter
Jane, aged fourteen.

The neighbourhood is rich in coal mines, and Hunter is a
collier's blacksmith, or more strictly, a blacksmith's striker His
trade brings in steady weekly earnings, but he is hampered with
old debts incurred to tradespeople who supplied him some years
ago with goods for the maintenance of a small shop for groceries,
bread and chandlery, which he used to keep at Whitestone. This
shop prospered well for a time, until he began to give credit to his
customers. During a strike of sixteen weeks at the pit the colliers
could pay little or nothing, and when they went to work again
many ignored their obligations. Mrs. Hunter complains that her
appeals to them were not seldom met by abuse and bad language,
instead of payment. Hunter was forced to give up his shop, but
would not go through the bankruptcy court. A neighbour whom
he highly respected advised him not to do so, telling him that he
would never hold up his head again if he did.

So he steadily continued to pay, and has now nearly cleared
himself, having been helped by the generous conduct of a Leicester
firm, which forgave him the last part of his debt. He had been
paying it off regularly in small fortnightly instalments to an agent
of the firm, who called to collect the money, when he had his leg
badly scalded in an accident at the pit, and was seriously ill for
some time. For several fortnights he could pay nothing. At last
he received a letter from the firm, but as both he and his wife are
poor scholars, they could not understand it, and feared that it
boded legal proceedings, or at least impatience for payment.
When the agent called next, however, he asked why they had not
answered the letter, and explained that the "gentlemen at
Leicester," being convinced of their good faith and genuine
inability to pay, had cancelled the remainder of the debt, a sum
of about £9.

Hunter's heart is not strong, and the doctor disapproves of his
continuing to work as a blacksmith, but he does not know what
else to do, and his wife is of opinion that the work does not "maul"
him so much as it would a man not used to it. She hopes, however,
that he may soon have a chance of returning to his old work of
sharpening tools for the colliers. This is lighter work, and is better
paid—3s. 8d. a day, and a small sum in addition, paid by the men
of each stall in the pit, as a sort of gratuity for having their tools

placed for them handily and in good order. The man who is at present doing this work is old, and talks of giving it up. If he does so Hunter may obtain his place.

The Hunter family is a large one. There are two elder sons married and away from home, and two married daughters in addition to the three young people still living with their parents. The sons married early, and though good and kind, have had their own families to see to, and were unable to aid materially in relieving Hunter from his load of debt. "The main help we have had is from the girls," Mrs. Hunter told me. The eldest seems to have delayed marriage for some time in order to be of assistance at home, and Mary, (aged twenty-five), intends to stay with her parents at least a year longer. By that time, they hope to be finally free of debt. The elder daughter also provided a home for William when at one time he worked at a distance from White-stone. She even did not wish to charge him for his board, but he insisted on paying her, so as not to be beholden to anyone.

William used to work on the pit bank, under his father and a married brother, who is also a blacksmith, but was not content with the wages, and has a fancy for a miner's work. He obtained it lately, as a collier's labourer*, at a pit which has been closed for some years, and is now re-opened. It is very wet. The water gains ground in spite of the pumps, and there are fears that it will have to be closed again. William was working for several weeks up to his knees in water, with the result that he was laid up with acute rheumatism. His ambition, however, is still to be a collier, and he has returned again to pit work.

Mary works at a neghbouring elastic factory. This work is hard, and as the factory is four miles distant from her father's cottage, the long walk before and after work is trying. She generally leaves home at five o'clock in the morning; but lately, whilst suffering from the effects of a severe cold, has been starting several hours later, apparently without losing her work, or getting into trouble with the manager.

Jane (aged fourteen), has left school, but does not go to work. She could have work at the elastic factory, but Mary dissuades her mother from sending her, saying that she is sure that Jane, who is delicate, could not stand it. So Jane helps her mother in the house, does a little "seaming,"† and looks forward to domestic service as her probable career.

Mrs. Hunter, from time to time, earns a little money herself by "seaming"† stockings and socks.

The only remaining source of income to the Hunter family came to an end last year. Mr. Hunter used to earn a little by selling hot peas on cricket grounds, or at neighbouring village greens, at fair time. But the machine for stewing the peas "hot and hot" is worn out, and it would cost 14s. 6d. to renew it.

The cottage occupied by Hunter is one of a row of four-roomed cottages. They are set a little back from the village street, and have small flower gardens in front, mostly well kept and gay with flowers in season. The Hunter's front door opens straight

---

* *cf.* note p. 53, "Some characteristics of Whitestone."
† See note p. 52.

into the sitting-room, full of small ornaments and pictures, with a sofa, several chairs, a side table, and that indispensable necessary of respectable cottage existence, a mahogany chest of drawers, with an antimacassar of crochet work on its top. The room, however, is generally fireless, and is not so comfortable as the kitchen, which has a good scullery out of it, and looks out on to a large piece of ground used in common by the inhabitants of this row for the drying of clothes. Beyond this again are the cottage gardens, with a good stretch of open country behind all.

The members of the family are all Primitive Methodists, and devote much time and thought to the concerns of their little chapel. There is no resident minister in the village, and the chapel is served on Sunday and on special week day occasions by one from a neighbouring town. The sect has a Sunday school, where Mary teaches regularly. It has an excellent reputation in the village, and numbers fifty scholars, members of other sects sending their children. The discipline enforced by the authorities of the Primitive Methodist communion is strict. It had been arranged last year that a childrens' treat should be celebrated by the Whitestone Primitives, on a particular date, but the resolution had been taken without any communication with the town centre, whose committee wrote a severe rebuke to Hunter, who was organizing the treat, and peremptorily ordered that the project should be given up. This decision reached Hunter only a day or two before the date fixed for the festivity, and it was extremely inconvenient to alter arrangements, and countermand supplies of food. But the order was obeyed with unquestioning submission.

The Hunters are not hostile to the Church. They welcome the clergyman's visits, and complain that they are so rare, excusing him, however, on account of his large family. They, and all the Primitive Methodists of Whitestone, are on excellent terms with the Wesleyan Methodists, who also own a chapel in the village. One of the crowning glories of the Wesleyan Harvest Festival last year was that all the Primitives were present, and were delighted.

The available household income at the disposal of Mrs. Hunter during the time covered by the accompanying accounts consisted of a weekly contribution of 10s. from William, of 7s. from Mary, and of a sum varying between 12s. and 14s. from Hunter himself. William and Mary clothe themselves, but their food (some of which they take with them to work) is entirely provided out of the money which they pay to their mother. I do not know the total amount of their earnings. Hunter earns 18s. a week, but keeps back some, out of which he pays regular instalments of the old debt, before spoken of. He works at a pit at a considerable distance from his own cottage, and has to lodge out from Monday till Saturday, paying 1s. a week for his room. He takes with him on his back on Sunday nights a loaf, some cocoa, butter and sugar, some raw meat or a made pie, and provides himself at the place where he spends his working week with any further food which he may require, some bread always, and sometimes extra cocoa and butter. Mrs. Hunter counts on being able to supply herself with potatoes and vegetables from the back garden, from Summer till Christmas.

After Christmas she generally has to begin to buy potatoes, till the new crop comes in again. The garden is in full yield now, which accounts for the absence of any payment for vegetables in the accounts. Fruit is bought from a travelling huckster who gives what a middle class housekeeper would consider very remarkable value in return for Mrs. Hunter's sixpence. For shoes and drapery, she also deals with "gentlemen who come round," and who are content to receive payment in small weekly sums, for goods supplied. Mrs. Hunter thinks that this plan costs a little more than paying ready money down, but says it is the only plan for poor people. She attends a mothers' meeting, where she is able to adopt a similar method, and pay gradually for goods ordered, but does not have them delivered to her till fully paid for. Coal can be had very cheaply in the village, which is near to several pits.

Every collier has a right to a load of coal weekly. In families where the father and one or two sons are colliers, the coal supplied is more than can be used, and is re-sold to neighbours at very reasonable prices. The death club, mentioned in the accounts, is one of long standing. The original undertaking intended to provide sick pay as well as £5 at death, and did so provide for a considerable time, but it has failed to attract new members, and is now reduced to a membership of six, Hunter being one. These six met last spring to consider their position, and finding the club funds very low, resolved to give no more sick pay, but to concentrate their efforts on the Death provision, for the present. They still do not give up hope of inducing fresh members to join; but it is not easy to share their confidence.

A sick club is subscribed to by both father and son, and I believe, provides 7s. a week in case of illness disabling from work. Two-pence a week is paid to the village doctor, who in return provides attendance, medicine, and surgical appliances, when necessary.

Why neither doctor's club nor death club received any money from Mrs. Hunter in the second week, I do not know. It will be seen that the sum put down for ale is only 4½d. in six weeks. I think Mrs. Hunter must have omitted to enter some payments. The expenditure for candles is mainly for candles used in the pit. In the statement of income and expenditure appended to the accounts, I have taken Hunter's contribution as 12s. a week. This was the minimum given by his wife, so that the sum unaccounted for is probably larger than 8s. 7d.

Six articles mentioned in the accounts were purchased more than once weekly.*

Bread was purchased 22 times in 6 weeks.			
Flour	,,	7	,, ,,
Butter	,,	9	,, ,,
Sugar	,,	8	,, ,,
Cheese	,,	7	,, ,,
Bacon	,,	8	,, ,,

* Milk is taken in daily, but paid for once a week. It is often contracted for for a payment of 6d. per week, giving about a pint daily.

During the period covered by the accounts, the prices current in the village for the main articles of food and common necessity, were as follows :—

> Bread, 5d. and 5½d. the quartern loaf.
> Flour, 5½d. and 6d. per quarter stone.
> Rice, 2d. per pound.
> Sugar, 2d. to 2⅓d. per pound.
> Butter, 1s. 3d., 1s. 4d. and 1s. 5d. per pound.
> Lard, 7d. per pound.
> Dripping, 4d. and 5d. per pound.
> Bacon, 7d. and 8d. per pound.
> Ham, 8d. and 8½d. per pound.
> Meat, 7d. and 8d. for mutton, 11d. for beef, per pound.
> Milk, 2½d. and 3d., skim milk 1d. a quart.
> Tea, 1s. 10d. and 2s. a pound.
> Coffee, 2s. a pound.
> Cocoa, 4d. a packet.
> Oil, 3d. a quart.
> Candles, 4¼d. a pound.
> Coals, 9d. a cwt.
> Tobacco, 3d. an ounce.

Note by Compiler, 1892 (28*b*).

Since 1891 no change has taken place in the *personnel* of the family, but the grown up daughter, working at an Elastic Factory, will shortly cease to be a member of it. She has put off her marriage for some time in order to help her parents to get clear of debt ; but is now preparing her trousseau and looks forward to marriage soon. Hunter has been able to do as he wished, and return to his old trade of tool sharpener to the colliers. He has now been three years with his present employer, where also a married son and the son still at home, are working. His hours of work are from six in the morning to five in the evening, with an interval of an hour for dinner. The wages are 3s. 8d. a day with the small extra sum earned for laying the colliers' tools in good order in their stalls. His expenses in connection with his trade are 3d. a week for his train on Saturday. On Sunday evening he walks back to his place of work. His tools are provided, with the exception of the hammer. He has used the same hammer for thirty years. His wife earns a little, at times, by seaming ; but she had none to do at the time of the second instalment of accounts (1892). The wages of Mary and William are irregular. The mother prides herself on never enquiring as to their total earnings. "They are always straight with me," she explained, Mary paying her 7s. and William 10s. a week with perfect regularity, and she asks no more.

The youngest daughter, who has left school but is delicate, still lives at home and helps her mother, who does not wish her to undertake any regular occupation until her health is better.

The hours of the family are very irregular, in consequence of the work its members have to do.

William gets up at four a. m. and pokes up the fire which has been banked up overnight for his convenience. He makes his tea for himself, eats bread and butter, or bread and bacon, or sometimes, if inclined, a " sop " which he concocts of bread, tea and milk, taking with him a little bread and cheese to eat at " snap " time, eleven o'clock.

In another hour Mary comes down, prepares for herself a similar breakfast, and starts for the Elastic Factory, carrying with her the materials for her dinner. Convenience for cooking anything she wants is provided at the factory. At about 8.30 a.m. Mrs. Hunter and her youngest daughter come down and breakfast. They take dinner together about one, and at 4.30 make ready William's dinner of meat and potatoes, early in the week. On Thursday, when the butcher kills, he generally has a piece of sheep's fry, and later, if all the meat bought at the beginning of the week is exhausted, he has bacon or eggs. Mary comes in later than her brother, and takes a meal, (tea and bread and butter). The mother and little sister take " a bite " either with her or William, as suits them best. After the little sister's bed time, Mrs. Hunter, Mary, and William sit down to a supper of bread and butter, cheese or cold bacon, between 8 and 9 p.m. When William is not at work, then Mrs. Hunter and he and Jane sit down to a regular dinner of meat and potatoes, at about one. On Sunday, the whole family take breakfast at about nine, dinner at one, and an afternoon meal of tea before Hunter leaves.

TABLES OF

INCOME AND EXPENDITURE.

Locality.	Occupation.	Number in Family. Males. No.	Males. Age.	Females. No.	Females. Age.	Weekly Average Income. £ s. d.	Weekly Average Expenditure. £ s. d.	Weekly Average Surplus or Deficit. s. d.	Accounts kept. No. of wks.	Accounts kept. Period.
London — Camberwell	Jobbing plumber	3	30, 8, 5	2	29, 3	0 11 7	0 11 6¾	+ 0 0¼	4	Feb., '91
,,	,,	,,	,, ,, ,,	,,	,, ,,	1 6 9	1 7 8¾	− 1 8¾	4	4 Apl.–1 May 1891
,,	,,	,,	31, 9, 6	,,	30, 4	0 14 11¾	0 14 9¾	+ 0 2	11	24 Sept.–9 Dec., '92
Stepney	Painter	1	51	3	34, 14, 8	0 19 10½	1 0 1	− 0 2½	10	Dec., '91–Feb., '92
Paddington	Painter's labourer	3	F. 16, 14	1	M.	2 1 3	1 19 4½	+ 1 10½	4	31 July–27 Aug., 92
	Assistant Relieving Officer	3	26, 3, 14 days	3	27, 1, 64	2 1 3	2 1 7¾	− 0 4¾	8	Sept.–Oct., 1891
	Dispenser	2	44, 8	4	39, 10, 6, 2	2 14 6½	2 3 9	+10 9½	14	Sept., '91–Jan., '92
	Soap-boiler	1	41	4	40, 12, 10, 34	2 6 6	2 9 8½	− 3 2½	4	June, '91
White-chapel	Journeyman slipper-maker	5	38, 11, 10, 6, 1	3	37, 8, 4	2 17 3¾	2 10 2¼	+ •7 1½	15	Sept.–Dec., 1892
Highgate	—	3	19 [13] 9	7	M, 23, 21, 17, 15 and 2 servants.	14 0 9½	14 0 7	+ 0 2½	52	[1892]
Provincial Towns — Liverpool	Carpenter	1	65‡	1	50‡	2 3 3½	1 17 10	+ 5 5½	22	Aug.–Dec., 1891
Manchester	Widow, & daughter, a machinist	—	—	2	66, 23	0 11 7½	0 11 3½	+ 0 4	8	Jan.–Mar., 1893
Manchester	Widow, and son, a hooker in a warehouse	1	18	1	M.	0 15 0	0 15 0	—	4	Jan., '93
St. Ives	Railway labourer	3	F, 2 sons	4	M, 3 daughters	1 0 0	0 16 0	+ 4 0	6	14 Aug.–Sept 25, '92
St. Ives	Fisherman	4	F, 8, 7, 4	2	M, $\frac{6}{12}$	0 10 10	0 9 3¾	+ 1 6¼	6	Aug.–Sept., 1892
Ashford	Railway foreman	3	54, 18, 11	3	52, 13, 8	1 5 6	1 8 6½	− 3 0½	16	Aug., Nov., Dec., '91, Jan., '92
Scotland	Artisan	—	F, 4 children,		M. 11, 7, 4, 2	2 8 0	1 17 0	+11 0	3	31 Jan.–21 Feb., '92
Scotland	Painter	3	F, 12, 9	3	M, 11, 8	1 7 10½	1 6 0	+ 1 10½	1	Jan. or Feb. 1892
Cambridge	Skilled assistant to a watch maker	1	F.	1 & servant	—	—	2 13 3½	—	52	Jan.–Dec., 1892
,,	,,	1	F.	3 & do.	M, sister, baby, servant, 14	—	2 14 8½	—	52	Jan.–Dec., 1893
,,	,,	1	F.	1 & do.	—	—	2 2 10	—	52	Jan.–Dec., 1894
Rural Districts Somerset	Agricultural labourer	3	45, 9, $\frac{6}{12}$	4	41, 13, 7, 5	0 11 6½	0 7 10	+ 3 8½	22	Nov., '91–April, '92
Somerset	Agricultural labourer	4	46, 19, 12, 6	4	41, 10, 8, 1	0 17 1½	0 12 2¾	+ 4 10¾	20	Nov.,' 91–April, '92
Somerset	Woodman and gardener	3	45, 9, 7	3	49, 5, 3	0 19 3	0 14 4½	+ 4 10½	2	1892
Surrey	Labourer and gardener	2	F, son	6	M, 5 daughters	[1 5 0]	1 1 11¾	+ 3 0¼	6	—
Surrey	—	—	—	2	80 [10]	—	0 3 6	—	6	—
Sussex	Journeyman carpenter	1	F.	4	M, 15, 13, 11	1 8 10½	1 4 10¾	+ 3 11¾	52	Jan.–Dec.,'92
Cumberland	Bobbin turner	2	30*, 3†	2	28, 5	1 12 1¾	1 9 0¼	+ 3 1½	52	Feb.–Feb., 1891
Leicester-shire	Bootmaker	2	F, 12	1	M.	15/- to 20/-	0 19 3¾	—	6	Aug.–Sept., 1891
,,	,,	2	F, 13	1	M.	15/- to 20/-	1 : 3½	—	6	Aug.–Sept., 1892
Leicester-shire	Collier	3	F, 19, 13	2	M, 4	1 6 0	1 5 7¾	+ 0 4½	6	Aug.–Sept., 1891
,,	,,	2	F, 14	2	M, 5	—	1 0 1½	—	6	Aug.–Sept., 1892
Leicester-shire	Colliery groom	3	F, 22, 17	3	M, 19, 13	30/- to 33/-	1 13 0	—	6	Aug.–Sept., 1891
,,	,,	2	F, 18	2	M, 14	15/- to 20/-	0 17 11½	—	6	Aug.–Sept., 1892
Leicester-shire	Colliery blacksmith	2	F, 22	3	M, 25, 14	1 9 0	1 9 0	—	6	Aug.–Sept., 1891
,,	Colliery tool-	2	F, 23	3	M, 26, 15	—	1 9 3¾	—	6	Aug.–Sept.,

SUMMARY.

Income for the whole period. Husband.	Wife.	Children.	Other Sources.	Total.	Expenditure for the whole period. Food and Drink.	Rent, Rates, Taxes.	Other Items.	Total.	No.
£ s. d.	£ s. d.	£ s. d.	£ s. d.	£ s. d.	£ s. d.	£ s. d.	£ s. d.	£ s. d.	
2 1 1	0 1 0	—	0 4 3	2 6 4	0 18 5½	0 16 0	0 11 9½	2 6 2¾	1*a*
5 7 0	—	—	—	5 7 0	1 16 4½	0 16 0	2 18 7¼	5 10 11½	1*b*
7 7 0	0 16 6	0 0 3½	0 1 0	8 4 9½	3 19 5¾	2 4 0	1 19 5¼	8 2 11	1*c*
—	8 6 3¼	—	1 12 6	9 18 9¼	5 11 0½	2 12 6	1 17 3½	10 0 10	2
5 5 0	0 12 0	2 8 0	—	8 5 0	5 10 1	1 4 0	1 3 4½	7 17 5½	3
15 0 0	—	—	1 10 0	16 10 0	10 14 7½	Free	5 18 6¾	16 13 2¼	4
38 3 8¼	—	—	—	38 3 8¼	21 14 9	Free	8 17 11	30 12 8	5
7 0 0	—	—	2 6 0	9 6 0	4 13 10	2 12 2	2 12 9½	9 18 9½	6
42 19 8¾	—	—	—	42 19 8¾	13 2 6½	7 0 6	17 9 10¾	37 12 11¼	7
—	715 0 0	15 0 0	—	730. 0 0	230 14 7	121 14 0	377 1 3	729 9 10	8
15 1 0	—	—	32 11 7	47 12 7	18 6 7	10 18 11	12 17 1	42 2 7	9
—	—	4 12 11	—	4 12 11	1 15 0	1 12 0	1 3 3½	4 10 3½	10
—	—	2 12 0	0 8 0	3 0 0	1 10 1	0 18 0	0 11 11	3 0 0	11
4 16 0	—	1 4 0	—	6 0 0	4 9 4	Not paid	0 6 9	4 16 1	12
3 5 0	—	—	—	3 5 0	1 17 1	0 5 0	0 13 9½	2 15 10½	13
20 8 0	—	Uncertain	—	[20 8 0]	13 7 9	2 1 6	7 7 4	22 16 7	14
6 9 0	—	—	0 15 0	7 4 0	3 5 11½	0 14 9	1 10 3¾	5 11 0½	15
1 4 4½	—	0 3 6	—	1 7 10½	0 15 11½	0 5 7½	0 4 5	1 6 0	16
Not known	—	—	23 8 0	—	48 6 7¾	16 0 0	73 9 10½	137 16 6¼	17*a*
,,	—	—	Board money for sister	—	56 14 6	20 0 0	65 10 9	142 5 3	17*b*
,,	—	—	—	—	51 8 4	20 0 0	39 19 6½	111 7 10½	17*c*
12 2 0	—	—	0 12 0	12 14 0	5 12 2½	Free	2 19 10½	8 12 1	18
11 15 0	—	5 0 0	0 7 8½	17 2 8¼	5 18 4	1 5 0	5 1 5	12 4 9	19
1 6 0	0 10 0	—	0 2 6	1 18 6	1 3 3	Free	0 5 6	1 8 9	20
7 10 0	Uncertain	—	—	[7 10 0]	5 8 1½	Free	1 3 9	6 11 10½	21
—	1 1 0	Uncertain	Garden	—	0 15 7	Free	0 5 5	1 1 0	22
70 4 0	—	—	4 17 0	75 1 0	29 17 2½	7 4 0	27 12 11¼	64 14 1¾	23
49 1 7	12 4 5½	—	22 6 0	83 12 0½	38 17 5	6 0 0	30 19 9	75 17 2	24
£5 to £6	—	—	—	£5 to £6	3 17 11	0 15 0	1 2 11½	5 15 10½	25*a*
£5 to £6	—	—	—	£5 to £6	4 4 10½	0 18 6	1 4 4½	6 7 9	25*b*
4 16 0	—	3 0 0	—	7 16 0	5 0 0	0 16 0	1 17 10	7 13 10	26*a*
Not known	—	—	—	—	3 13 1½	0 18 0	1 9 7½	6 0 9	26*b*
£2 14/- to £4	Uncertain	[6 10 0]	—	—	6 18 5	0 16 0	2 3 8	9 18 1	27*a*
£2 14/- to £4	,,	[2 0 0]	—	—	3 18 6¼	0 9 0	1 0 3¼	5 7 9½	27*b*
3 12 0	—	5 2 0	—	8 14 0	5 0 6	0 15 0	2 18 6	8 14 0	28*a*
—	—	—	—	—	5 3 4	0 15 0	2 17 6	8 15 10	28*b*

No.		Average Weekly Expenditure on Food and Drink.	Bread.	Flour and Biscuits.	Other Cereals.	Butter.	Lard, Dripping, Suet.	Meat.	Bacon.	Fish, Poultry.	Milk.	Eggs.
		£ s. d.	s. d.	s. d.	s. d.	s. d.	s. d.	s. d.	s. d.	s. d.	s. d.	s. d.
1	a	0 4 7¼	0 11	0 2½	0 0½	0 4	0 1½	0 8¾	0 0½	0 6¾	0 3	0 0¾
	b	0 9 1	1 6	0 3	—	0 8	0 1	2 2¾	0 2	0 6½	0 5¾	0 3½
	c	0 7 2¾	1 7	0 3	0 1	0 5	0 2½	1 7¾	0 2¼	0 7	0 5¼	0 1
2		0 11 1¼	2 3¼	0 2½	0 1	0 8¾	0 1¼	3 4½	0 2¼	0 1½	0 9¼	0 1¾
3		1 7 6¼	2 4½	0 6	0 7	2 4	0 4½	5 3½	0 3½	1 6½	1 1	0 9½
4		1 6 10	2 6½	0 5	0 5½	1 8½	0 3¼	6 6	3 0¼	1 1	2 2¾	0 3
5		1 11 0½	1 11½	0 2	0 5½	2 8¼	0 2	6 7½	0 3	5 2½	2 11	2 0
6		1 3 5½	4 0¾	0 6½	0 11¾	2 4	1 1¾	2 6	—	0 1	2 6	1 0
7		0 17 6	4 4	0 3¾	0 1¼	1 3½	0 1	2 7½	—	1 1	1 5	0 4½
8		4 8 9	6 6		Included under dried fruit, etc.	Included under cheese	Included under cheese	20 0	Included under cheese	3 0	11 0	—
9		0 16 8	0 10	0 10	0 1½	1 1¾	0 2½	4 8¼	1 2¼	0 11½	1 1½	0 5
10		0 4 4½	0 8¾	0 0½	0 0¼	0 9	0 0¼	1 0½	0 2½	—	0 4½	0 0½
11		0 7 6¼	1 8¼	0 1¾	—	0 8	—	1 10¼	0 4¼	—	0 4½	—
12		0 14 10¾	0 4¼	3 10½	0 2½	2 3½	0 5	5 1	0 6½	—	—	—
13		0 6 2	0 8½	2 2	—	1 8	—	0 10	0 0¼	—	0 0¾	—
14		0 16 8¾	4 8¼		0 0¾	1 9	0 2¾	4 0¾	0 2½	0 2	1 8	0 5¼
15		1 2 0	2 5	1 8¼	1 3¼	2 8¼	—	2 4	—	0 10¼	2 8¾	1 6¼
16		0 15 11½	3 9	0 6¼	0 9½	1 5½	0 1½	2 6	0 5	0 3	2 2	0 5½
17	a	0 18 7	2 1¾	0 3½	0 1¾	0 8¾	0 2¾	5 3½	1 9	0 9½	1 2	1 3½
	b	1 1 9¾	2 2½	0 10¾	0 2¼	1 2¼	0 3	6 0	1 6½	0 8¾	2 6¾	0 2
	c	0 19 9½	1 10½	0 8¼	0 4	0 11¼	0 2½	5 4	1 3½	0 10	1 11	1 4½
18		0 5 1¼	1 8	0 3½	0 0¾	0 2½	0 2¼	0 1	0 11¼	—	0 0½	—
19		0 5 11	2 0	0 6¼	0 0¾	0 3¼	0 3¼	—	1 1	—	0 1¾	—
20		0 11 7½		3 1½	—	1 2	—	—	3 2½	—	0 3	—
21		0 18 0½	5 7¾	—	—	1 1	1 1¾	5 2	1 3	—	1 2	—
22		0 2 7¼	0 10		0 1	¼-lb. given	0 3¼	—	0 2½	—	—	0 2
23		0 11 5¾		2 8¾	0 1¼	1 10½	0 6¾	2 2	—	0 0¾	1 0	0 1¼
24		0 14 11½		2 11½	0 1¾	1 10¾	0 7¾	3 6¾	1 0	0 2	0 10¼	0 6¼
25	a	0 13 0	1 9	0 6	—	1 4	0 1	3 9½	1 0	—	0 10½	0 6
	b	0 14 1¾		2 5¼	—	1 4¼	0 2	4 1	0 10	—	1 0	0 7
26	a	0 16 8		2 9½	0 c¼	1 7	—	6 8	1 0	0 2	0 6	0 0½
	b	0 12 2¼		2 0	—	0 6¼	—	4 1½	2 3½	—	0 5¾	0 1½
27	a	1 3 1	4 11¼	1 2	—	4 2½	0 8	6 3¾	2 2½	—	—	—
	b	0 13 1	2 6¾	0 5	—	2 7½	0 6	3 8¾	0 0¾	—	—	0 4½
28	a	0 16 9	2 8	1 1	0 1¾	1 8½	0 2¼	4 8¼	1 4¼	—	0 6	0 3
	b	0 17 3	2 5	1 0	0 1¼	0 11½	0 5¾	5 9½	1 5	—	0 5	—

Other Vegetables.	Fresh Fruit.	Dried Fruit.	Sugar.	Jam, Treacle, etc.	Condiments.	Meals out.	Tea.	Coffee, Cocoa, Non-Alcoholic Drinks.	Alcoholic Drinks.	No.
s. d.	s. d.	s. d.	s. d.	s. d.	s. d.	s. d.	s. d.	s. d.	s. d.	
0 2	0 0½	0 0¼	0 3½	0 1	0 0½	0 2	0 4¼	0 0½	—	1a
0 3	—	0 0¼	0 3¼	0 1¾	0 0½	0 10¼	0 5¾	—	0 4	1b
0 4	0 0½	—	0 4½	0 1½	0 1¼	0 0½	0 4½	0 0½	0 0¼	1c
0 5¼	—	0 1¾	0 5½	0 3	0 1	—	0 7¾	0 3	0 4	2
0 8	0 4¾	—	0 7½	—	0 0½	5 2½	2 0	0 0¾	2 3	3
0 10½	0 8½	0 1	0 11¾	0 0¼	0 1¼	—	0 8	0 7½	3 2¼	4
0 11¾		—	0 10	0 2¾	0 1	—	0 10¼	0 6½	3 9	5
1 11½	1 11½	0 6	1 0	0 3½	0 1¼	—	1 6	—	—	6
0 3¼	0 5¾	0 1½	1 1	0 8¼	0 1¼	—	0 5½	0 7¾	1 0½	7
9 0			20 6			6 9	Included under	dried fruit, etc.		8
0 6¼	0 5	—	0 7	0 1½	0 2½	—	1 2	0 6½	0 4½	9
0 0½	—	—	0 2½	0 0¾	—	—	0 4½	0 0½	0 0½	10
0 2½	—	—	0 10½	—	—	1 2¼	0 1¾	—	—	11
—	—	0 3¼	0 3¼	0 8½	0 1½	—	0 8¼	—	—	12
—	0 1¼	0 2½	0 1¼	—	0 0¼	—	0 3¼	—	—	13
	0 4¾	0 4¼	0 10	0 2½	0 1½	—	0 6½	0 3¾	—	14
0 5¾	0 4	0 1½	1 3¾	0 10¼	0 0¾	—	1 0¼	1 6¾	—	15
0 2	—	0 4½	0 10	0 9½	0 1	—	0 9¼	—	—	16
2 4½		0 2½	0 9¾	0 5	0 2½	—	0 7½	0 3½	0 2½	17a
1 11¾		0 2¾	1 2	0 4½	0 2½	—	0 6½	0 3	0 10¼	17b
1 6¾		0 3	0 10½	0 5	0 3	Unclassified grocery 0 8*	0 3¼	0 2¾	0 4¾	17c
Garden	Garden	0 0¼	0 1¼	0 1¾	0 0¼	—	0 3¾	0 0½	0 0¼	18
0 0¼	"	0 1¾	0 2	0 2¼	0 0½	—	0 3½	—	—	19
Garden	"	0 5	0 7½	—	0 1	—	0 11	—	—	20
"		0 6¾	0 5	—	—	—	0 8	0 1¼	home-brewed ale	21
"	Garden		0 3	—	0 1	—	0 6	—	—	22
—	0 1	0 1¾	0 10½	0 0¼	0 0¾	—	0 8½	0 3	—	23
0 1	0 2¾	0 1¾	1 0¼	—	0 1½	—	0 11	0 0¾	—	24
Garden	0 3	0 3½	1 2¾	—	0 2¾	—	0 6	—	—	25a
"	0 9	0 4¼	1 2½	—	0 2½	—	0 6	—	—	25b
"	0 5½	0 2½	0 11½	—	0 0¼	—	0 11	—	1 0	26a
"	0 3	0 1	0 4	—	0 1¼	—	0 6	0 1	0 10½	26b
"	Garden	—	1 8½	—	0 0½	—	0 7	0 1	—	27a
"	"	—	1 2¾	—	0 1½	—	0 7	0 1¼	—	27b
"	0 5	0 1	1 2¾	—	0 1¼	—	1 1¼	0 3½	0 0¾	28a
"	0 11¼	0 2¼	1 2½	—	0 2¼	—	0 8½	0 3½	—	28b

* Sums paid for grocery. Particulars not given.

C **EXPENSES OTHER THAN**

No.	Total Average Weekly Expenditure.	Rent, Rates, Taxes.	Fuel.	Light, Matches.	Furniture and House Utensils.	Washing and Cleaning Materials.	Clothes.	Boots.	Travelling.	Service.	Recreation.
	£ s. d.	s. d.	s. d.	s. d.	s. d.	s. d.	s. d.	s. d.	s. d.	s. d.	s. d.
1 a	0 11 6¾	4 0	1 0¾	0 2¼	—	0 3½	—	1 2	—	—	—
1 b	1 7 8¾	4 0	1 4¾	0 2	0 11¼	0 3¼	1 4	2 10½	—	1 5¼	—
1 c	0 14 9¾	4 0	1 3¼	0 2¼	0 1¼	0 4¼	0 6	0 9½	0 1¼	0 0½	—
2	1 0 1	5 3	1 6	0 5	—	0 4	—	0 1¼	—	—	0 1¾
3	1 19 4½	6 0	1 3¾	0 3½	0 4½	0 8¾	0 8¼	0 0½	0 10¼	—	0 6
4	2 1 7¾		Free		0 0¾	0 2	1 0½	0 6	0 4¾	2 6¾	0 5
5	2 3 9		Free		—	0 3½	3 5½		--	1 7	0 11½
6	2 9 8½	13 0½	6 4	0 6¾	2 0	1 0	—	0 7	—	0 1	0 6¼
7	2 10 2¼	9 4½	1 2	0 11½	0 2	1 6½	1 2	0 11¼	—	—	—
8	14 0 7	46 9¾	6 1¾	4 6½	7 10¾	Included in service	17 4		7 0	31 2½	7 7½
9	1 17 10	9 11¼	1 6¼	0 8	2 1½	1 2¼	1 9	—	—	0 2½	—
10	0 11 3½	4 0	1 1¾	0 2	0 0¾	0 2	0 1¼	0 1¾	—	0 2½	—
11	0 15 0	4 6	2 1½	—	—	0 0½	—	—	—	—	—
12	0 16 0	Not paid	—	0 2	—	0 4½	—	—	—	—	—
13	0 9 3¾	0 10	0 10½	0 1½	—	0 1½	—	—	—	—	—
14	1 8 6½	2 7¼	2 0¼	0 5	—	0 8	1 1¾	1 5¼	—	—	0 1¾
15	1 17 0	4 11	1 2	0 7¼	—	0 10¼	2 6		—	—	0 5
16	1 6 0	5 7½	0 11½	0 4	—	0 5¾	—	—	—	—	0 3½
17 a	2 13 3½	8 1	1 7¾	0 7	4 10	0 4½	5 8¾	0 5¼	0 4	2 7¼	2 2½
17 b	2 14 8½	7 8¼	1 7	0 9	1 0	0 7½	5 3¼	0 4	2 1¼	5 2½	—
17 c	2 2 10	7 8¼	1 11	0 6¼	1 5	0 7½	2 10¼	0 6¼	0 4¾	3 3	1 11¼
18	0 7 10	Free	0 1½	0 2½	0 1½	0 1¾	1 2¾	0 3¼	—	—	0 0½
19	0 12 2¾	1 3	1 1¾	0 1¾	0 0¼	0 1¾	1 0¼	1 3¾	—	—	—
20	0 14 4½	Free	1 0	0 2¼	—	0 2¾	0 4	0 9	—	—	—
21	1 1 11¾		Free		—	0 3¾	—	0 5½	—	—	2 6
22	0 3 6	Free	Free	0 1¼	—	0 2	—	0 3½	—	0 2	—
23	1 4 10¾	2 9¼	1 2¾	0 6½	0 5¾	0 2¾	4 2	1 1¼	0 0¾	—	0 0½
24	1 9 0¼	2 3¾	1 2½	0 2¼	2 1¾	0 4	5 8	—	—	—	0 2¼
25 a	0 19 3¾	2 6	2 3¼	0 4½	—	0 6	—	—	—	—	—
25 b	1 1 3½	3 1	2 3¼	0 5¼	—	0 5¾	—	—	—	—	—
26 a	1 5 7¾	2 8	0 4	0 9	—	0 4¼	1 9¾	0 4	—	—	0 2
26 b	1 0 1½	3 0	0 4	0 6	0 3	0 3	0 9¾	0 7	—	—	0 1
27 a	1 13 0	2 8	2 0	0 8½	—	0 3	1 3	1 11	—	—	—
27 b	0 17 11½	1 5	1 2	0 2¾	—	0 3	0 5	0 8	—	—	—
28 a	1 9 0	2 6	1 4	1 0	0 6	0 6¼	2 0	1 0	—	—	—
28 b	1 9 3¾	2 6	1 5	1 0¼	0 8	0 4¾	2 11½	1 0	—	—	—

FOOD—Weekly Averages. C

Education.	Religious Observances.	Charity and Gifts.	Pocket Money.	Pet Animals.	Insurance.	Tobacco	Health Medicine and Drugs.	Expenses of Industry.	Loans	Repayment of Loans.	Other Expenses.	No.
s. d.	s. d.	s. d.	s. d.	s. d.	s. d.	s. d.	s. d.	s. d.	s. d.	s. d.	s. d.	
0 2¼	—	—	—	—	—	—	0 c½	—	—	—	—	1 a
0 8¼	—	—	—	—	—	—	1 4½	--	—	4 1¾	0 0½	1 b
—	—	—	—	—	—	—	0 1½	—	—	—	0 1	1 c
..	—	0 1	0 3¾	0 3¾	—	0 2	0 3	0 1¼	—	—	—	2
—	0 1	0 3	—	0 1¼	0 3	—	—	—	—	—	0 3¾	3
—		0 3¾	—	0 1½	0 4¾	0 6	3 9¼	—	—	4 6½	0 0½	4
—	2 0	0 4	—	—	3 9½	—	Free	—	—	—	0 4	5
0 4	—	0 3	—	0 4¾	0 9	—	—	—	—	—	0 4¾	6
—	—	0 0¼	1 7¼	0 0¾	0 1	—	0 0½	13 9	—	1 10	—	7
40 2¼	4 11	3 4¾	2 9	—	—	—	7 11¼	—	—	—	4 1	8
—	—	—	0 6½	0 3¼	—	0 5½	0 3½	—	1 4¾	—	0 10	9
—	—	0 0½	—	—	0 4	—	0 6	—	—	—	0 0½	10
—	—	—	—	—	0 6	—	0 2	—	—	—	0 1¾	11
—	—	—	—	—	0 3	0 3	—	—	—	—	0 1	12
—	—	—	—	—	—	0 5½	—	—	—	0 5	0 3½	13
0 4½	—	—	—	—	1 10½	—	0 11¼	—	—	—	0 2	14
—	1 7	—	—	—	2 11¾	—	—	—	—	—	—	15
0 1½	0 7¼	0 1	—	—	0 11½	0 7	—	—	—	—	—	16
—	0 9¼	0 3¾	—	—	4 0½	—	1 6¼	—	—	—	1 2¼	17 a
—	0 9	0 6¼	—	—	4 7¼	—	0 9¼	—	—	—	1 8¼	17 b
—	—	0 7¼	—	—	—	—	0 2	—	—	—	1 1½	17 c
—	—	—	—	—	0 3¼	—	—	0 3¾	—	—	0 0½	18
—	—	—	—	—	—	—	—	1 3¼	—	—	—	19
—	—	—	—	—	—	—	—	1 0	—	—	—	20
—	—	—	0 6	—	—	—	0 2¼	—	—	—	—	21
—	—	—	—	—	—	—	0 2	—	—	—	—	22
—	—	0 1¼	0 10¾	0 0½	1 2½	—	0 0¾	0 4½	—	—	0 1	23
0 6½	—	0 3¼	—	—	—	—	0 10¼	—	—	—	0 4¾"	24
—	—	—	—	—	0 8	—	—	—	—	—	—	25 a
—	—	—	—	—	0 10½	—	—	—	—	—	—	25 b
—	—	—	—	—	1 11½	—	—	—	—	—	0 7¼	26 a
—	—	—	—	0 0½	1 2	—	0 0¾	—	—	—	0 10½	26 b
—	—	—	—	—	1 0	0 2	—	—	—	—	—	27 a
—	—	—	—	—	0 6	0 1¾	—	—	—	—	—	27 b
—	—	—	—	—	1 8½	—	—	—	—	—	1 8	28 a
—	—	—	—	—	1 10¾	0 3	—	—	—	—	—	28 b

D PERCENTAGES OF EXPENDITURE.

(a) As a whole.   (b) On food and Drink.

No.	Total Average Weekly Expenditure.	Food and Drink.	Rent, Rates and Taxes.	Other Items.	Total.	Average Weekly Expenditure on Food and Drink.	Bread and Flour.	Meat.	Other Food.	Tea.
	£ s. d.					£ s. d.				
1 a	0 11 6¾	39·81	34·59	25·60	100	0 4 7¼	23·9	16·7	50·7	7·7
1 b	1 7 8¾	32·76	14·42	52·82	100	0 9 1	19·3	26·4	45·5	5·3
1 c	0 14 9¾	48·80	27·01	24·19	100	0 7 2⅝	25·4	25·4	43·2	5·2
2	1 0 1	55·29	26·14	18·57	100	0 11 1½	22·3	32·1	34·5	5·8
3	1 19 4½	69·89	15·24	14·87	100	1 7 6¼	10·4	20·3	53·7	7·2
4	2 1 7¾	64·43	Free.	35·57	100	1 6 10	11·0	35·5	36·8	2·4
5	2 3 9	70·95	Free.	29·05	100	1 11 0½	6·7	22·2	54·5	2·7
6	2 9 8¼	47·19	{ 26·24 / 21·76* }	26·57	100	1 3 5½	19·6	10·7	63·3	6·4
7	2 10 2¼	34·87	18·68	46·45	100	0 17 6	26·5	15·0	46·2	2·6
8	14 0 7	31·63	{ 16·69 / 12·33* }	51·68	100	4 8 9	7·3	22·5	70·2	—
9	1 17 10	44·05	{ 26·27 / 19·23* }	29·68	100	0 16 8	10·0	35·2	42·2	7·0
10	0 11 3½	38·74	35·42	25·84	100	0 4 4½	17·6	28·6	43·4	8·6
11	0 15 0	50·14	30·00	19·86	100	0 7 6¼	24·4	29·4	44·3	1·9
12	0 16 0	93·10	Free.	6·90	100	0 14 10¾	28·4	37·8	29·2	4·6
13	0 9 3¾	66·22	8·95	24·83	100	0 6 2	46·6	13·8	35·2	4·4
14	1 8 6½	58·62	9·12	32·26	100	0 16 8¾	28·0	25·5	41·4	3·3
15	1 17 0	59·42	{ 13·31 / 9·91* }	27·27	100	1 2 0	18·7	10·6	59·0	4·6
16	1 6 0	61·21	21·63	17·16	100	0 15 11½	26·8	18·3	50·1	4·8
17 a	2 13 3½	35·06	{ 15·25 / 11·20* }	49·69	100	0 18 7	12·4	35·9	45·6	3·4
17 b	2 14 8½	39·87	14·05	46·08	100	1 1 9¾	14·2	34·6	43·6	2·5
17 c	2 2 10	46·21	18·00	35·79	100	0 19 9½	12·9	33·4	49·1	1·4
18	0 7 10	65·16	Free.	34·84	100	0 5 1¼	38·4	20·0	34·3	6·1
19	0 12 2¾	48·38	10·22 ·	41·40	100	0 5 11	42·6	18·3	34·2	4·9
20	0 14 4½	80·86	Free.	19·14	100	0 11 7½	26·9	27·6	37·6	7·9
21	1 1 11¾	81·99	Free.	18·01	100	0 18 0¼	31·3	35·6	28·8	3·8
22	0 3 6	74·40	Free.	25·60	100	0 2 7¼	32·0	8·0	40·8	19·2
23	1 4 10¾	46·11	11·13	42·76	100	0 11 5¾	23·8	18·9	49·0	6·1
24	1 9 0¼	51·28	7·97	40·75	100	0 14 11½	19·6	30·2	43·6	6·2
25 a	0 19 3¾	67·31	12·95	19·74	100	0 13 0	17·3	36·9	42·0	3·8
25 b	1 1 3½	66·24	14·48	19·28	100	0 14 1¾	17·2	34·8	44·5	3·5
26 a	1 5 7¾	64·99	10·39	24·62	100	0 16 8	16·8	46·0	25·7	5·5
26 b	1 0 1½	60·56	14·91	24·53	100	0 12 2¼	16·4	52·6	19·0	4·1
27 a	1 13 0	69·95	8·08	21·97	100	1 3 1	26·4	36·9	33·8	2·5
27 b	0 17 11½	72·85	8·36	18·79	100	0 13 1	22·8	29·0	43·0	4·4
28 a	1 9 0	57·76	8·62	33·62	100	0 16 9	22·4	36·1	32·8	6.6
28 b	1 9 3¾	58·85	8·53	32·62	100	0 17 3	19·8	41·8	32·6	4·1